HIGH LEVEL WARFARE

Safe from Counter Attack

Voice of The Light Ministries

HIGH LEVEL
WARFARE

Safe from Counter Attack

Dr. Ana Méndez Ferrell

Voice of The Light Ministries

High Level Warfare, Safe from Counter Attack

© Dr. Ana Méndez Ferrell

5th Edition revised and increased 2018

The Biblical references from the original text in Spanish are quoted from Reina Valera, revised in 1960.

The Biblical references from the translation to English are quoted from The King James Version , King James and International Version.

Category: Spiritual Warfare

Printing: United States of America

Published by: Voice of The Light Ministries
                     P. O. Box 3418
                     Ponte Vedra, Florida, 32004
                     United States of America

www.VoiceOfTheLight.com

ISBN: 978-1-944681-24-1

DEDICATION

I dedicate this book, first of all, to my heavenly Father, Jesus Christ and to the Holy Spirit. Secondly, to my spiritual parents on earth, Dr. Morris Cerullo and his wife Teresa, who gave birth to me in the spiritual warfare ministry, who trained and anointed me, so that God could transform me into who I am now, one of His conquering generals.

Also, to my close combat team, who have given their lives at my side in the most powerful battles we have fought: Flory González, Liliana Torres, Mary Corona and my husband Emerson Ferrell.

COMMENTARY

T he church is called to new levels of warfare rarely experienced throughout its 2000 years of history. Nevertheless, a vocal anti-war movement is rising, proclaiming that Jesus Christ has not given us authority against the enemy. I do not know of anyone who is better qualified to address this situation than Ana Mendez Ferrell.

Ana clearly traces the paths we should walk using an accurate knowledge of the Bible, molded by intense personal experiences, not only in the invisible world but in the realm of darkness and the realm of light, as well.

This book is essential for every serious Christian worker.

C. Peter Wagner
Chancellor, Wagner Leadership Institute

CONTENTS

Introduction

"I have commanded my sanctified ones, I have also called my mighty ones for mine anger, even them that rejoice in my highness. The noise of a multitude in the mountains, like as of a great people; a tumultuous noise of the kingdoms of nations gathered together: the Lord of hosts mustereth the host of the battle."

-Isaiah 13:3, 4

God is carrying out a powerful recruiting of His troops to fight the battles that will liberate the nations from the yoke of the devil. For this reason, He is leading His church into a clearer understanding of what it means to wage spiritual warfare in the heavenly realms.

In order to fight at these levels, it is necessary to understand foundations and principles of warfare that will allow us to emerge unscathed from it.

I write this book based upon deep revelation and

extensive personal encounters in the realm of spiritual warfare. I believe not only theology is necessary but also the experience of pioneers who have paid the price. In addition, this understanding will give us a solid base on which we can emerge victorious from combat.

It is my opinion that those who have experienced the dangers, errors and strategies of war and have won, are the ones who are the most qualified to bring light on the subject.

In all the great movements of the Holy Spirit, the devil has raised up an opposition among those, who have never experienced a profound revelation of what God is doing. Nevertheless, those opponents "have strong opinions."

King Saul had a "strong opinion" on how to defeat Goliath with his heavy armor, but the real wisdom and anointing to do this was experienced by tiny David. This is not an exception in spiritual warfare and has caused great damage to the kingdom of darkness.

For this reason, I find it practical to write and instruct on high-level warfare in the heavenly regions, in order to bring about security and courage that are needed to see the warfare accomplished.

It is possible to emerge victoriously without devastating retaliation from the enemy, but there are rules of engagement we have to observe and understand.

On these pages, you will find revelations that are not commonly heard in the body of Christ; this is the fruit of a life immersed in God for the purpose of destroying the works of the devil. Also, on these pages you will find errors committed during the pioneering years. These errors were necessary in order to train the army of God.

Also you will find profound reflections on warfare that can only be obtained after innumerable battles and victories.

I believe God has inspired this book so that His light can (will?) shine upon all the questions raised by courageous warriors. These are questions that books on theology are unable to answer; valid questions emerging from the voices of confusion unleashed by the devil in an attempt to discourage the true warriors.

May God enlighten the eyes of your understanding as you read these pages, and may you be inspired to enlist in the earthly army of the living God!

The Army of God

Paralyzed by fear

"For God hath not given us the spirit of fear; but of power, and of love, and of a soundmind." 2 Timothy 1:7

S ince the nineties began, we have begun to see, as revealed to us by God, the growing development and fuller understanding of spiritual warfare. God began to remove the veils from Scripture, enabling various prophets to have an understanding of how demonic powers and principalities are structured and how they operate in the heavenly realms. In addition, the Lord has continued to give wisdom on how to tear down these strongholds in the Spirit realm. He opened a heavenly door that will transform homes, cities and nations. All of this has given birth to a powerful army around the world, which is beginning to disturb the kingdom of darkness, bringing tremendous advancement for the Kingdom of God.

By the grace of God, I am a member of this army, assigned to be one of His generals. Thanks to God's indescribable power, I have been able to win territories while waging glorious battle in some of the darkest places on the earth. We have fought numerous wars in the heavenly places against powerful demonic spiritual strongholds, bringing freedom to millions of people who were without hope, trapped under the terrible yoke of demonic oppression. We have seen awesome awakening in regions where it was practically impossible for the gospel to penetrate. These regions were sentenced to live as pastoral cemeteries. The dark forces of the enemy had gripped the church and placed it in a state of lethargy, almost without hope.

In the majority of nations who are governed by extreme demonic powers, most churches do not know how to defend themselves against the assaults of the devil. The enemy has torn and continues to tear them asunder daily, while millions of people are dragged into hell.

In His infinite mercy, God began to lift up an army of courageous and uncompromising people, who are willing and committed to lay down their lives for the Lord, even unto death. They have dared to confront the powers of wickedness so the gospel can penetrate and save millions of lost souls. After seeing the powerful results from these genuine battles directed by God through His true prophets, many are inspired to follow in our footsteps. Some have accomplished it successfully, while others, unfortunately, have become victims of serious misfortunes.

The reason for these misfortunes is that not every Christian is called to fight on the frontline. In addition, others who are called have yet to understand the proper way to keep themselves safe from the devil's attacks. There have also been some brothers who were motivated by their own emotions, who chose to act outside the order of established authority, and, who launched their own battles against these territorial powers and came out wounded from these battles.

The results of these ignorant combat initiatives have prompted the devil to counterattacks creating more disaster than blessings. But the major disadvantage of all is that the enemy uses these mistakes to release a powerful wave of fear upon the church and against spiritual warfare. The devil's strategy is to paralyze the true army of God and impede the advancement of the gospel throughout the nations so that we never come into total freedom and deliverance.

Unfortunately, various prophets, pastors and leaders, bombarded with the negative consequences unleashed by these misinformed people, are closing their doors to the rising up of the army of God. This is understandable; however, this confusion, ignorance and fear are not from the Lord. They are from the devil, who has a well-planned strategy to win the war. There are a multitude of pastors rising up to prevent the destruction of demonic strongholds in the second heaven. They do not pause to think that the war is not going to cease just because the army of God has been detained. The devil is not going to sit back with his arms crossed, nor ignore the church just because the church does not want to fight. Have we not heard a thousand times that he only comes to rob, kill and destroy? It is much easier to plunder an unguarded house without defenders in the outer gates, than it is to attack a house equipped with powerful weapons, shields, and armies.

Under the pretext that "it is better to be safe and conservative" (in which I was a profound believer), satan has infiltrated the army of God with his powerful spirits of terror in order to paralyze and dissolve it. If this wave of terror begins to subside, it is because the enemy has suffered irreparable damages and is trying to stop us by using all necessary tactics and means at its disposal.

New theologies are emerging in many places, telling the body of Christ that our Lord did not give us power to fight against principalities and dominions in the heavenly realms and that if they try, they will become victims of terrible tragedies.

Theology must be based on the Word of God, not on the negative experiences of those acting out of their ignorance and disorder.

Our Lord gave me the grace and means to travel to a great number of countries throughout the world. I have heard the voices of many marvelous intercessors that God wants to enlist for the purpose of dismantling the works of the devil, thereby establishing our Lord's reign over the nations. Regrettably, the rumors and books containing new ideas and theologies have inspired fear, leaving these intercessors intimidated and confused. The glory of God is not being carried into the lesser-evangelized regions of the world; because the army of God is paralyzed with fear, thinking that they will suffer misfortune and tragedy, if they enter into spiritual warfare. The great harvest is not advancing, nor are these doctrines regarding the reign of God being carried to the darkest locations on earth.

It is easy to say to people: "Do not engage in spiritual warfare" in those regions that have been evangelized for centuries. Yet as we sing our "Hallelujah's" in our beautiful sanctuaries, there are people in Africa, Latin America, Asia, Europe and the United States being torn to pieces by the devil's strongholds. Powerful territorial spiritual powers of witchcraft destroy our brothers and the only thing they hear is "Do not wage war." They live without power and hope and are exposed to the devil's desires and mercy.

There are pastors who come to me saying, "My church is very small; we are in an area that is full of witches. These malignant spirits have entered my home and picked up my son, throwing him against the walls. He is a child surrendered to God; we have no idea how to defend ourselves." I have visited churches established right in the middle of spiritual power lines (called ley lines) where these territorial spirits render them to bits. They are laden with sicknesses, adultery and filthiness because no one knows how to confront the devil.

On one occasion, a very powerful church in Colorado Springs called saying: "We have been invaded by death. One after another our senior members have died and there have been dreams and visions where our senior pastor has died. We don't know what to do."

This church was constructed over an ancient Indian cemetery; the territorial spirits demanded their lives as payment for profaning their shrine. If we had not gone to war in the heavenly realms against this territorial principality, their pastor would now be dead.

On another occasion, we had an experience in Uganda, which filled me with a divine wrath and that became the last straw that led me to write this book. We arrived to the city of Masaka, which was dominated by a sorcerer from a neighboring mountain.

Upon meeting with the pastor who invited us, we saw that something was terribly wrong. His countenance was haggard and his voice denoted a stifling burden. He began to tell us how the warlock along with his people, was killing one brethren from the church per month. "We are desperate and terrified," he told us with tears in his eyes, "we don't know what to do and we suffer thinking of who the next victim will be."

He then added as he showed us a popular book: "The worst part is that we have no hope left. They taught us that it is very dangerous to wage spiritual warfare. This book was sent to inform us about the misfortunes that happen to the warriors who attempt it. What do you think sister? Are we to allow ourselves to die without doing anything?"

"Of course not", I furiously retorted outraged at such asinine doctrine. "Let us put an end to this matter. Our team will confront this sorcerer and he will find out who is the one true God."

We waged an extremely powerful war that concluded in an encounter such as the one of Elijah and the priests of Baal on Mount Carmel. God manifested Himself very powerfully, defeating the warlock. Half of his people converted to Christ.

The result of that battle did away with the deaths and changed the spiritual atmosphere in the whole city. Street violence ended and the government repaired and beautified the city.

The discouragement and fear of waging strategic spiritual warfare under the threat of tragic counterattacks, the confusion of the warriors and the surrender of arms are not the fruit of a doctrine that comes from God. On the other hand, and in this I rejoice, these doctrines are pulling off from the frontlines of battle those who should never have been there in the first place. It is much better for these people to remain under the protection and will of God doing the work that He has set before them in the body of Christ.

This does not mean the devil will not attack them. Every Christian should be armed and be aware of the enemy's schemes. No one is exempt from these attacks emerging out of the second heaven. When these attacks happen, I do not believe anyone can say to satan: "I'm sorry, but I don't pick fights against principalities in the second heaven." Brothers, at the moment, it is much better to be prepared because it is not we, the Christians, who are initiating the fires of attack. The devil is in our territories shooting in every direction, destroying our societies and dragging millions into hell (including your loved ones, unless you begin to fight for them), long before there was any talk about spiritual warfare.

I perceived from God to write this book, not with the intention of attacking anyone but to undo the wave of fear and confusion launched on God's true army. My longing is to open your eyes to the truth God wants you to know, resulting in boldness, courage and an authentic warfare anointing on those who are called to be part of this glorious army and who want to fight together with Christ.

I bless those who have tried, with sincere hearts and good intentions, to protect the people of God from unnecessary errors. Always remember: "We do not fight against people made of flesh and blood, but against the evil rulers and authorities of the unseen world, against those mighty powers of darkness who rule this world, and against wicked spirits in the heavenly realms."

This is the testimony I want you to hear from one of God's generals, one who has fought against principalities, powers and dominions of darkness at the highest level in the heavenly regions, winning without suffering the casualties of War.

I intend to make an incisive analysis to bring an understanding of how powerful spiritual warfare is won in the second heaven. I also want to illustrate how to win within the authority and might of Christ, eliminating unnecessary errors. This book is not based on the experiences of others, but on the vast experience and understanding of the spiritual world I have come to know through God's grace and favor.

My sincere and profound prayer is for the army of God to be lifted up with great valor so that we will wage combat together in the wisdom of the Most High until that day when the world is filled with the knowledge of the glory of God.

2

Who is Ana Méndez?

"Jesus said unto him, if thou canst believe, all things are possible to him that believeth."　　　*Mark 9:23*

This is the testimony of how God rescued me from being a voodoo priestess when He called me to His service.

I was eighteen years old when Jesus Christ appeared in my room. It was at night and the sky was cloudy due to the rainy season. I was in my bedroom preparing for a final exam when something distracted me from my studies. I began to have an impression that an extremely powerful force was attracting me towards the window. Curiously, I stood up and went to see what this force that drawing me was.

How great was my surprise to see a marvelous light

shining in the middle of those clouds! It was like a huge gigantic star, something I had never seen before in my life. I waited for several seconds trying to figure out what this could be. Suddenly, a very intense light broke away from the star and entered my window, filling the room with extreme brilliance.

I fell to the floor as if I was dead. I could not lift up my head nor move any part of my body. I could not stop the tears that began to flow from my eyes. My heart could not bear being in the presence of such indescribable love and goodness. A strange combination of feelings stirred within me. I felt filthy and insignificant, and at the same time I felt-like the most fortunate woman in the universe.

Suddenly, I stopped noticing what was around me. I was enveloped in marvelous ecstasy. I did not know what was happening but my eyes saw our Lord Jesus Christ in all of His majesty. I was submerged in the wisdom and knowledge of God. During this experience, I was able to see how all knowledge co-existed and was revealed. Nothing was hidden from me.

Our Lord spoke and awkwardly I wrote it on a piece of paper. I cannot recall how many hours went by. Little by little, the vision began to vanish and I found myself flat on the floor, bathed in tears with a sheet of paper in my hand that read: "I am Jesus Christ, your Lord. I have come to tell you that within time, I will make myself known to you, because you are My servant; I will come to you through a man with blue eyes."

From that moment on I fell profoundly in love with Jesus. From there I began my most desperate quest to encounter Him again and to serve Him. During that time, Christian churches were unheard of in Mexico at least where I grew up. They were not found in the circles in which I moved. I was brought up as a Catholic, so my search was in the only place I could think of, the Roman institution.

Shortly after my encounter with Jesus in 1974, I went to live in France. While I was there, I decided to attend mass and take communion every day. I did this for two years without the slightest manifestation of His presence.

I remember going to the parks and telling people how important it is to seek Jesus because He is our Savior. I was insulted and humiliated many times but I knew it was true and that the world just had to know this. I was not aware that I needed to read the Bible because this was prohibited by the Catholic Church in Latin American countries; only priests were allowed to read it. The persecution by Parisians who did not understand me, and the coldness and close- mindedness of the Roman church, were extinguishing the flame inside me until one day I decided Jesus was not to be found in those places. I stopped attending mass and started to seek Him in other areas. It was then I decided to immerse myself in oriental religions, which presented an "avatar" named "Jesus." I wanted to find Him no matter where He happened to be. After two more years of yoga and meditation, I became aware that this marvelous Jesus was not to be found in their philosophy.

It was at that time someone told me that such an encounter could only be found through the illuminated ones. This was an experience only a few people had the privilege to know, and if I was chosen, they could help me. They gave me information regarding a man who apparently had these qualities. This is how I came to know of a powerful warlock of a most high order; he was very intellectual and well versed in the knowledge of the most profound currents of the occult.

His conversation appeared so fascinating to me. He spoke about God, the universe, magical powers and other worlds that took my breath away. I spoke to him about my search for Jesus and His kingdom, my yearning to know Jesus in a supernatural and powerful way, and not just the Jesus who was dead and continuously displayed on a crucifix on the Catholic altars. He smiled in an enchanting way and told me that he definitely was the one who could help me.

He picked up a Bible and opened it to John chapter three, where Jesus spoke to Nicodemus regarding being born again. He said: "It's necessary for you to be born again to enter into the Kingdom of God, this is the kingdom of magic and the supernatural. In order to do this, we have to deliver your spirit to death since no one can be born again unless they have died to the useless and material things of this world. It is through the understanding of death that you will be able to penetrate and acquire the marvelous life of Jesus." The open Bible and the hope of encountering Jesus were sufficient enough to deceive me. Due to my ignorance, it was there that I fell into the most terrible and diabolical trap of my life.

We planned my initiation ceremony largely based on the sacrifice of animals from the book of Leviticus. It was necessary for the person, who would be initiated, to be bathed in the animal's blood. This, according to him, represented the blood of atonement. When I arrived at the home of the sorcerer, dressed in my white ceremonial clothes, I found him waiting for me clothed in a long black robe with a red collar. His assistant was also dressed in a long black robe.

In the middle of the living room I could see a long table covered with a black cloth and a candle placed on each corner. A statue of Saint Teresita, Patroness of Death, was placed at the head of this table. To one side of the table prepared in advance was a fireplace with two canes and the "govies" (these are covered ceramic pots within which dwelt helping spirits). The canes were the medium through which the spirit of death could communicate as explained to me by the sorcerer. At the other side of the table there were many statues of saints and virgins positioned as if they were observing the ceremony. This did not cause any restlessness within me because they were the same statues I had seen in the Roman church. Accompanying me were my three maidenly assistants, assigned to help me and be with me during the whole ceremony.

The moment arrived; a beautiful symphony by Wagner began to play. This kind of music is part of the magical seduction. The dark side of the spiritual world not only has the strident sounds of rock and roll, but also has the kind of music that fascinates the senses, lifting one into a sublime fascination where every fiber of the soul is felt. These are strategies of the devil, designed to make us lower our guard in order to subtly penetrate and possess the incautious soul. There was expectation in the air, something powerful captivated and forced us to proceed.

The warlock began evoking spiritual forces to enter into action. Later, after a series of spells, he took bread and wine and gave them to me as a symbol of the pact. Little by little he began to transform into a different presence, which now spoke through him, keeping the same fascinating tone.

He picked up the birds we had brought for the sacrifice, two roosters and two white doves. With the blood of the roosters, he began to bathe the images of the saints and virgins, and invoked over them the names of the African gods that each one represented. Later, he gutted the doves and dripped the liquid of their entrails over me. This signaled my maidens to assist me in the removal of my clothing in another room, after which they wrapped me like a mummy for the funeral celebration. After I was enveloped in the funeral strips of cloth, they carried and placed me on the table covered with the black cloth, which represented my coffin.

The warlock proceeded to read the catholic liturgy for the dead, invoking the spirit of death to come over me. He ended saying: "Ana Méndez, rest in peace!" Then, he turned out the lights; the candles on the four corners of my coffin cast the only light in the room. I remained alone in that room together with my maidens. I could not move due to the burial strips of cloth. I was equally filled with fear and another strange emotion I had never felt before.

For a long time, the only sound we heard was the "tic-tock" of the clock. Suddenly I felt a force that possessed me, and in that instant, I found myself outside my body, floating in the middle of the room. At that moment, the canes leaning against the fireplace began to straighten up by themselves, softly thumping the floor as if they were in a march. I observed all of this in a stupor as I floated above when a figure of black smoke with extended bony hands suddenly began to emerge out of the statue of Saint

Teresita. Her face was that of a cadaver. Her hair was long and tangled. With her sharp nails she began to open up a trail on my body, which was lying on the table. I wanted to scream at her to stop, but from my floating position, I was unable to do so. In seconds she disappeared inside my body and I couldn't see her. Later, other figures came out of the fireplace. Their visage was made of a pale green smoke and they too entered my body.

At that instant, I returned to my flesh. I could feel a very strong power in every cell of my body. I felt like a battery loaded with high-tension electricity. The magnetic force within me attracted the canes and they formed a cross on my chest; two invisible bird claws took possession of my brain. One of the maidens gave a deep long scream declaring: "They are pulling out my soul, they are taking me." The sorcerer quickly entered the room and proceeded to direct the new birth while his assistant attended to the maiden. In a symbolic gesture, he mimicked the delivery of a baby from its mother's womb, in this way; he removed me from the table. He then said: "Now you are born again. You have been born into the powers of magic." And he proceeded to give me my initiated name.

We came away from the ceremony and I was no longer myself. I was now totally possessed by a force that controlled my steps in the occult world. Terribly deceived, my soul had entered into a pact with the devil. Certainly, no one ever told me that the one I had entered into alliance with was satan. They believe that what they practice is inoffensive white magic and not the black magic practiced by the followers of Lucifer. The sorcerer declared, "We have an alliance with the spirits of light, who come from our saintly brothers and the virgins, whose mission is to help us with our walk here on the earth." Little by little, I came to realize that this was untrue. The phrase that resounded within me said: "Once you are on this path, there is no exit."

I began to work with the warlock. Our work was in hexes, fetishism reading cards and enrolling as many people as we could into witchcraft.

The voices of the spirits who had possession of me became clearer. They were very powerful. They had the capacity to heal the sick and perform exorcisms, which was deceitful because, we would remove one devil but then introduce many others in its place. The poor person would go away happy thinking he had been delivered.

Within a short amount of time the warlock became aware of my strong magical abilities and he invited me to form a triangle of power along with another witch who was a friend of ours. The ceremonies became even stronger. Each time we performed more sacrifices with larger animals. The spells and devils possessing us became more and more powerful as we increased in power. We entered cemeteries at midnight, on nights with a full moon; we pulled out of the grave the spirits of the dead so that they would become our allies. Accesses to the spiritual world and visitations from messengers disguised as angels of light were the bread of our daily existence. The power that came from me (or the devils inside me) had more and more impact.

My personality was noticeably transformed. My heart was filled with hate for all people. I became an extremely violent person, with such incredible strength that even men were surprised. I was filled with arrogance and contempt towards others. I developed a thirst to kill. I never killed any humans, thanks be to God, but I did enjoy sacrificing the animals. For me, this had evolved into a drug as I sensed the power that came out of them during their death throes.

As I increased in knowledge and as I was elevated into the different levels of the occult, the devil began to manifest in me. What began as visits from an incredibly beautiful being which came to instruct and seduce me to be his wife, turned later into the real, ugly and horrible being he actually is. His subtlety in the beginning was fascinating and enchanting, but then his manner transformed into tyranny; I had to obey whatever he demanded.

Any resistance resulted in immediate torment from devils that came to whip me. My house was completely haunted. Ghosts entered, exited and lived continuously in my place. I spent entire nights consumed with terror by spirits who had been assigned to torment me until I was exhausted.

On the other hand, I was favored with fame, money and influential friends. However, I began to notice something that did not fit with everything satan bragged about himself. I had already been initiated into the position of high priestess of voodoo magic, something akin to Palo Mayombe (the highest grade achieved by Cuban Santeria). This allowed me to approach the high satanic hierarchies and even the devil, asking whatever I needed to perform my magical work. However, I found out that, no matter how great the sacrifice or ceremony performed, there were things the devil simply could not do.

This began to happen quite often. I began to suspect all the power he bragged about was actually limited. There were areas he simply could not enter and people he could not touch. This made me very angry towards him, because in many ways, he boasted more of his powers than he was actually able to accomplish. When he finally became aware I knew something about him that nobody was allowed to know, he decided to kill me.

One evening, when the sorcerer and I went to the witches market in Mexico to acquire the necessary supplies for a ceremony, he told me: "I want to introduce you to the Patron of Misery. This is the name of the principality who rules this place." We entered into various nooks and crannies of that market; however, the place with a crystal niche was empty when we arrived.

With an air of frustration, he let out a sigh and later added: "What a shame, they've taken him out to eat." (This means they removed him to offer a blood sacrifice.) "I wanted you to see him because he is very impressive. It is the figure of a child, but it has no eyes. It has hollow cavities and blood that runs down from them over his cheeks."

We left the market arriving back at the area where our car was parked. The warlock started to scream at me: "Look, look, there at the side of the car, the side next to you." I had not seen anything next to the car but I turned again anyway to see what was there. Much to my surprise I saw a beggar writhing on the ground in a spot near the door where there was nothing before. The warlock continued to raise his voice with great excitement: "Look, his eyes! It's him! It's the patron! Listen!" He continued, "He wants to tell us something."

I was paralyzed with terror, unable to take my eyes away from him. A voice came out of him, from spirit to spirit saying: "I have come to you to reclaim what belongs to me." He then disappeared from our sight.

We remained speechless. We both knew he wanted

both our souls in hell, but neither one of us dared to confess this to each other. After this day, death came upon us, like something that had attached itself to our shoulders. Every day it would repeat to each of us: "I'm coming for you. It is your hour."

During that entire year I witnessed the most horrendous and deadly attacks. First, while visiting El Salvador where some of my family resides, I fell ill with a horrible strain of pneumonia and was admitted to the hospital. There was a war going on in El Salvador at that time. One night the city was bombed and one of the bombs landed near the hospital.

Shortly thereafter, in Los Angeles, California, two armed men assaulted me with the intention of raping and killing me, but I knew the hand of God intervened. These men threw me into the street after beating me, but it did not go any further than that. Two months later, they arrested these men and found out they had murdered seven people in the same neighborhood.

Then, a propane tank caught fire in my apartment. I had to extinguish it with a blanket and my own body while the devil screamed at me: "You're going to die!"

Shortly after this, a terrible earthquake measuring 8 points on the Richter scale occurred in Mexico City. Over 300,000 people perished. My apartment was located in the disaster area along with hundreds of other buildings that were totally destroyed. When I went out trying to rescue those who were still alive, trapped under rubble, the building exploded. Once again, the hand of God saved me from burning in the fire by letting me escape miraculously.

The voice of the devil spoke even louder and more frequently: "I'm coming for you. You belong to me. You're going to die." The tension became stronger. My nerves, along with all the demons that resided in me, were destroying me. My health began to fail and nervous breakdowns began to beat me down.

I decided to fly to Puerto Rico for a rest when a torrential rainstorm caused a landslide on a mountain near the area where I was staying. Once again, corpses surrounded me, people trapped under debris. It was here that I experienced a partial facial palsy because of my deteriorating psychological condition and of the extreme tension.

That year I lived through extreme forms of pain. I learned the soul can anesthetize itself when suffering reaches a point you feel you cannot go on. It is a point of rupture, an inner tearing. I am using the word tearing because literally, I felt as if claws were tearing me from the inside. At these times I entered into a state of numbness where I no longer felt anything for long periods of time until the pain appeared again. The pain was stronger than before whenever it reappeared. The devil took me into the deepest chambers of hell where I could see lost souls, burned and whipped at the destructive glee of their tormentors. Once I entered into one of the tunnels of death and saw bodies stretched up for miles in different stages of decomposition. I also saw faces that have been contorted by desperation and impotence, which tried to detain me in that place of eternal darkness. I know well what the word darkness means; it is when life no longer appears to have even the slightest ray of hope and when one finds no escape from anguish, loneliness and sadness.

I returned to Mexico, trying to find a way to end my torment. However, in addition to all the torments, I found myself subjected to a violent attack when all the demons living in me rose up to kill me at the same time. The fight raged fiercely within me; and when I finally could not stand it anymore, I tried to take my life by cutting my wrists.

I had already lost much blood when my twin sister arrived at my apartment. She took me to the hospital. There in the emergency room, balancing between life and death, the unexpected happened, a glorious presence began to descend over me and in the middle of it, there was an audible voice, which said: "Your Father in heaven will not abandon you." It was the same light I had seen in that first visit when Jesus came to me. I was filled with inexpressible peace.

I woke up in a room of the psychiatric wing of the hospital 48 hours later due to sedatives. I was in a separate building protected by security bars surrounded by many mentally ill patients. I was not an exception; I was one of them, and was in the worst condition of them all. I remember my mother was at the foot of my bed when I opened my eyes. The first thing I said to her was: "Mom, there's going to be such a strong manifestation of God in this place that it's going to change all of our lives." My mother, a confirmed atheist and a follower of Nietzsche, thought it was all part of a hallucination and did not pay any attention to me.

After several tests, the doctor came to the conclusion that my case was very serious. He thought the safest plan was to confine me for a long time, but God had other plans. After a few days my beloved aunt, Gloria Capriles, whom I had not seen for several years, arrived. She was a beautiful and very sweet lady, full of love and compassion. She told me about a man who had changed her life and she wanted to bring him to the hospital so I could meet him. I said yes, more out of curiosity than faith.

The next day she returned with a Christian pastor with blue eyes (At that time, this detail from my previous vision was buried in the abyss of my madness). Meanwhile, he gave me the message of salvation and I listened attentively. Something inside of me said every word spoken by this man was the truth.

Regardless, my reaction was to weep with intense sadness as I told him: "What a terrible thing! You are preaching to me the salvation of my soul. I know what you are saying is true, but in spite of this, I cannot run to Jesus. I have made pacts with satan that cannot be broken any attempt to break them will bring all the fury of the devil into my life."

In that moment of profound grief, the minister interrupted me by saying: "This isn't true! The Word of God says: 'If we confess our sins, He is faithful and just and will forgive us our sins and purify us from all unrighteousness.'" The blood of Jesus breaks every pact! Our Lord Jesus died for you to free you from the chains of the devil."

Those words caused an earthquake to shake within me. Without a doubt, the Holy Spirit was present; he was working deeply within my soul. "What do I have to do to receive Jesus in my heart?" I asked him with tears in my eyes. I had an utmost desire for my beloved Jesus Christ to put an end to my interminable nightmare. "Repent, ask Him to come and dwell in your heart, and tell Him that you want Him to be your Lord and Savior," he said.

I found it very difficult when I heard the word "repent." This was the hardest thing for me to do. The Holy Spirit came over me in that instant convicting me so strongly of my sin that I broke down in a mixture of pain and shame.

It was a repentance, which instantly purged my conscience.

My soul literally poured out before God, crying out for His mercy. It was in that profound and true prayer when the Holy Spirit removed the veils from my eyes that I saw with all clarity the deception in which the devil had led me. "Forgive me Lord, forgive me..." I said in a weak voice. It was frightening to think that He with His beautiful purity was looking at the horrible person I had become. No one could have felt as filthy and wretched as I did in that hour. I desired with fervor to touch His impeccable goodness and take back everything I had lost when I became separated from His light.

The demons of anger and destruction moved within me. It was a wicked battle and my whole being was involved. "Pull me away Lord, from these worms that are consuming me!" I cried out in desperation from deep within my being. I continued confessing my sins, without any pretense. I could see exactly how I had served the devil and how each one of my actions nailed Jesus to the cross. Each one of my sins was like a direct confrontation to the purity and sanctity of God. In spite of this, He still loved me and gave His life for me. No one was less deserving of His grace, His mercy, and, His forgiveness than I was.

The presence of God was overwhelming. I felt like a disgusting worm before His divinity. As I confessed, I felt within my being a fire that was consuming me. I deserved pain of torture and death more than the pretentious indulgence I aspired for. "Lord!" I screamed. "I'm not worthy that you should even listen to me. But who else is capable of having mercy upon me, except you? I'm dying, my Father, in all ways I am broken and my heart is in pieces."

In that instant, I felt His love began filling me. I could clearly sense He was forgiving me. I could not believe there was such a love that could have compassion on me. On Me! A servant of satan! But He did. I said to Him with all of my strength and being: "Thank you Lord Jesus! Enter now into my heart and take my hand so I will never be apart from you again; be my Lord and my Savior!"

As I finished speaking, the pastor placed his hands on my head and said: "Lord, I beg you clean your daughter Ana from all wickedness, break all of the pacts she has made with the devil." I had the impression I was seeing Him at that moment nailed to the cross, telling me He had done this because of His love for me, so I would be redeemed. It was so real I could almost touch Him. I could see the blood running down His body, taking with it the burden of all the sins of the world. He spilled His blood in order to give me life while I in exchange, had thrown away mine towards destruction.

Christian, the pastor, continued praying:"And I ask you, right now, in this moment, all indwelling spirits be cast out. I invite the Holy Spirit to come upon her." There have never been simpler words. In that precise instant, it felt as if a lightening bolt had fallen from the skies and broke all of the chains binding me. I felt as if it was breaking all of the pain, suffering and anguish out of my heart that used to oppress me, smashing them all into a million pieces. The room was filled with an indescribably beautiful light, and I felt again that wonderful goodness which had been present the first time Jesus visited me. I felt like a bird that could fly away at any moment. My heart filled up with peace and joy. Of one thing I was sure; Christ had made me completely free.

During the days I spent in the hospital the presence of God was very strong in my life. The first thing the Holy Spirit told me was not to backslide in even the smallest way because the enemy was furious with me due to my decision to follow Christ. Far from feeling any fear, I was instead filled with a divine passion to make war against the devil until the very end. I wanted to take back from him all of the souls I could possibly save and to bring to light all of his deceptions. I wanted to set the captives free and serve God with all my heart.

I was profoundly grateful for my salvation. The words Jesus spoke are so true when He said: "Those who have received the greatest pardon are the ones who loved the most." (Note: this seems to be a quotation from Luke 7.42-47 which says the one who is forgiven much, is the one who loved much.) No matter what, there was something that kept turning somersaults in my head and I could not understand what it was. I inquired within my spirit. "Jesus, you came to me when I was 18 years old. You knew I fell deeply in love with You at that time. I was insulted because of Your name when I tried to be Your messenger. I would have served you with my entire being. Why Lord, in eleven years, did You not send anyone to me who could show me Your path? Why did You allow me to fall into the hands of the devil in such a deceptive way as it happened? Why did I have to live through all of those horrible nightmares at the hands of satan, if You knew how much I loved You and I was searching for You?"

His love enveloped me one more time and he spoke into my heart: "It was necessary for you to live in the profound miseries of the devil for the purpose I have called you to do in your life. I never left you nor abandoned you, nor did I let him kill you as he wanted to do. I wanted you to know the weaknesses of the devil and his limitations so you would lose your fear of him, and to understand the weaknesses of the human heart and the lies of his ministry. I am going to use you in an immense way to free cities and nations from the destructive works of the devil."

This testimony is much larger, longer and dramatic than what I have stated in this chapter. However, I can tell you that since the day of my salvation, the reign of darkness has been shaken and torn down many times. I have seen the devil several times and he knows that I know he has no power. It is we who have the power through Christ Jesus. When the devil becomes aware you know he is a defeated foe, you truly become an enemy he greatly fears.

3

Spiritual Warfare in the Right Perspective

"Finally, my brethren, be strong in the Lord, and in the power of his might. Put on the whole armour of God, that ye may be able to stand against the wiles of the devil. For we wrestle not against flesh and blood, but against principalities, against powers, against the rulers of the darkness of this world, against spiritual wickedness in high places." Ephesians 6:10-12

a) A Just War

I have heard several servants of God say that the church has no cause to fight against the devil and his demons because "The war belongs to God" and He is the only one who can fight against these hierarchies of darkness. They also say that the fighting done by God's children in this type of high-level warfare is not of God. Nothing could be more false or misunderstood than what I have just narrated. You will clearly see for the following reason.

The first thing we need to understand is that the devil, in all of the supposed power some people want to credit him with, is no more than a creature and on top of that, a fallen creature. Compared to God, he is no greater than a fly and with just a puff of His breath, God can easily disintegrate him. If it were God's plan to do battle all by Himself, the devil would have disappeared a long time ago.

Think for a moment how infinitely powerful God is. The earth and its entire splendor is only a footstool at His feet. He created by His word all of the universe and the heavens within heavens that cannot contain Him. Scripture, speaking about Him and all of His great wonders says:

"The LORD reigneth, he is clothed with majesty; the LORD is clothed with strength, wherewith he hath girded himself: the world also is established,

that it cannot be moved. Thy throne is established
of old: thou art from everlasting. The LORD on
high is mightier than the noise of many waters,
yea, than the mighty waves of the sea."

-Psalms 93:1, 2 and 4

It also states:

"The hills melted like wax at the presence of the
LORD, at the presence of the Lord of the
whole earth."   *-Psalms 97:5*

There is nothing that can compare itself to His power and glory. Among the qualities that make Him infinitely great is that He is infinitely just. He is incapable of doing anything unjust. For this reason, it is impossible for God to go into a face-to-face combat with the devil. It would be a very unjust war, for a powerful God to fight against such a tiny fallen creature. Since this was impossible, God pre-planned how to destroy him and yet, receive all the glory for doing so.

God's plan was to have someone who was made just a little lower than the angels, be the one who would defeat him. For this reason, Jesus, His only Son, humbled Himself, became a man and "came to destroy the works of the devil." (1 John 3:8; NLT 2007).

"Thou madest him a little lower than the angels;

*thou crownedst him with glory and honour, and
didst set him over the works of thy hands: Thou
hast put all things in subjection under his feet.
For in that he put all in subjection under him, he
left nothing that is not put under him. But now
we see not yet all things put under him."*

Hebrews 2:7, 8

What a grand and glorious plan, to destroy the devil
with a creature made just a little lower than the angels!
Jesus Christ, God made man, defeated the devil on the
cross at Calvary, not just for a time but for all time,
categorically and absolutely destroying his empire. From
the highest in authority to the lowest and darkest regions
of his reign, he was defeated. Now this does not mean, as
some might think, that this is the end of it all, that the case
is closed and that there is no need to fight.

*"But this man, after he had offered one sacrifice
for sins for ever, sat down on the right hand of
God; From henceforth expecting till his enemies
be made his footstool."*   *Hebrews 10:12, 13*

Yes, He is waiting and expecting His enemies to be
made His footstool; it can be clearly understood then that
someone else must put His enemies in that position, and
the Church is the one to do it.

"And to make all men see what is the fellowship

of the mystery, which from the beginning of the world hath been hid in God, who created all things by Jesus Christ: To the intent that now unto the principalities and powers in heavenly places might be known by the church the manifold wisdom of God."   Ephesians 3:9, 10

We must understand that all the victories of the cross are perfect and absolute. God however, has delegated to the Body of Christ, His church, and those things that need to be accomplished on the earth. We analyze this as such: "Jesus died to save all men! This occurred at the cross and it is irrevocable, but it does not mean all men are automatically saved. The church must still preach the Gospel and the unredeemed still need to accept it.

Another victory of the cross is Jesus taking all of our illness, disease and sorrows upon Himself. This is absolutely true. The church must still pray and receive healing by faith; otherwise, nothing happens.

Another truth is Jesus defeated above all else the power of the devil, but it doesn't mean the devil no longer exists and the church no longer has to do anything about him. As we have just read, the body of Christ has to announce to the powers and principalities in the heavenly places that Jesus conquered him at the cross and has to take authority over them.

Certainly, it is Christ in us who fights our battles and in this way, the power of God is unleashed upon the devil.

God acts on behalf of the righteous on the basis of their prayers. The more authority, anointing and understanding a prayer warrior has in his prayers, the greater the intervention of God will be. God simply uses man as His channel through which He sends His power.

In the Old Testament, the greatest war in which God manifested His power through the use of a man was in the deliverance of Israel from its captivity in Egypt. In this war, Jehovah did not do anything unless it was through Moses. The courage and obedience of this great servant who confronted Pharaoh and the Egyptian gods were determining factors in the deliverance of Israel.

> "Surely the Lord GOD will do nothing, but he revealeth his secret unto his servants the prophets."   -Amos 3:7

"For Mine is the battle." This means that the Holy Spirit reveals to His servants, the prophets, the strategies and the Word that must be declared in order to win. This unleashes the power of God upon principalities and strongholds, and the saints get the victory. It isn't up to us to declare: "God, we leave everything up to You. We must deal with the forces of darkness in the second heaven."

b) War in the Heavenly Regions

1. - How do you describe the spiritual world?

When we speak of spiritual warfare, we not only need to know the strategies of our enemy, we must also know the territory in which the battle is to be fought.

The Bible speaks very clearly to us about this battleground:

> *"Finally, my brethren, be strong in the Lord, and in the power of his might. Put on the whole armour of God, that ye may be able to stand against the wiles of the devil. For we wrestle not against flesh and blood, but against principalities, against powers, against the rulers of the darkness of this world, against spiritual wickedness in high places."*   *-Ephesians 6:10-12*

There is currently an opinion circulating within the body of Christ which says that Jesus, to whom all authority and power in heaven and on earth was given, gave His church authority only on the earth. This opinion says that under no circumstance do we have any authority over what is known as the second heaven or the spiritual realm where the devil operates because only God can do battle in these regions. This is true in a sense. However, He will not act unless there's a corresponding prayer on earth.

The truth is that this type of thought, which is inspired by dreams and human conjectures, is nothing more than a spirit of error that has infiltrated the church and which has no Scriptural foundation with that it could be proved.

Let's analyze these thoughts from a Biblical point of view. Let's look at the translation from Ephesians 6:12 from various versions.

"...hosts of wickedness in the heavenly places." (ASV)

"...Spirits of Wickedness on High." (Twentieth Century New Testament)

"...spiritual hosts of evil arrayed against us in the heavenly warfare." (New Testament Weymouth)

"...Spiritual agents from the very headquarters of evil." (J. B. Phillips New Testament)

"...against mighty powers in this dark world, and against evil spirits in the heavenly places." (New Living Translation)

"...Spirit forces of wickedness in the heavenly (supernatural) sphere." (Amplified Bible)

"...ritual forces that control evil in the heavenly world." (God's Word Translation)

In all of these different translations, we see a coherent view that warfare takes place in a spirit realm where the devil moves and operates. Nowhere in Scripture do we see God making a difference between an "earthly" spiritual realm and a "heavenly" demonic spiritual realm, as if there is an invisible line that divides them!

The earthly world is the material realm and the spirit world is the invisible realm. A demon may inhabit a physical body, but that does not make it an earthly creature. It still belongs to the invisible world and must be dealt with, spiritually.

When the Apostle Paul referred to the hosts of wickedness in the heavenly realms, he is referring precisely to spirits that inhabit and operate through human hosts. Nevertheless, he says these spirits must be dealt with in the spiritual realm, or in heavenly spheres. There is no fundamental difference between "higher" or "lower" realms in which the powers of darkness operate, because in reality these powers operate in one single realm.

Many people think that a believer has the right to fight a power of darkness that presents itself to him here on earth. But if the powers are in the second heaven the believer no longer has the authority to fight against it. I declare that this idea shows a poor understanding of the invisible world. The heavenly realm does not have dividing limits between a lower and higher section. It's a dimension different from ours, but it operates in our midst.

As a prophet of God and as a general in spiritual warfare, I have also seen this many times when I used to belong to the enemy's army before my conversion. It is a dimension that has diverse regions: places of captivity and bondage, areas of torment, strongholds of demonic government, wells of imprisonment, deserts, and areas of deep darkness. The powers of darkness are able to move in all directions: from side to side and up and down. All of this takes place in the midst of our earth. If we try to understand all of this with our natural minds, asking how can a second heaven (above) and another one in the world (below) exist together, confusion is inevitable. Spiritual things have to be discerned spiritually. Let's see an example to clear up that there is not an above and a below in the spiritual world.

One of the most powerful dominions ruling the earth is the "Great Prostitute" of Revelation, also known as the "queen of heaven." The Word says,

> *"The woman you saw is the great city that rules over the kings of the earth."*
>
> Revelation 17:18. (TNIV)

Where is this great city? Is it below on the earth or above in the second heaven?

The Word says she sits over many waters and these waters are towns and nations. Is this above or below? It also says she is in the desert.

In Revelation 17:3 it reads:

"So he carried me away in the spirit into the wilderness: and I saw a woman sit upon a scarlet coloured beast, full of names of blasphemy, having seven heads and ten horns."

Did John go up to the second heaven, or, was the woman on the earth? It tells us,

"With whom the kings of the earth have committed fornication, and the inhabitants of the earth have been made drunk with the wine of her fornication."   *(Revelation 17:2)*

Where did they fornicate and drink the wine? Was it in the second heaven or, is the city that rules over the world found on earth and not in the second heaven? If we don't have authority in the celestial realm as some say, then where? God says:

"Reward her even as she rewarded you, and double unto her double according to her works: in the cup which she hath filled fill to her double. How much she hath glorified herself, and lived deliciously, so much torment and sorrow give her: for she saith in her heart, I sit a queen, and am no widow, and shall see no sorrow."

Revelation 18:6, 7

Is she going to descend from the second heaven so we can torment her or do we have to rise and go to her?

Don't complicate your life by pondering a question that makes no sense. The truth is that there isn't a second heaven, which exists above, somewhere, who knows where, in which horrible and inaccessible demons do their foul deeds in some spiritual region. The devil operates in a spiritual realm without any intermediary divisions. This is an invisible world that the Apostle Paul referred to when he spoke about heavenly realms or the spiritual world. You may call it the second heaven if you so desire, but it is important to know that it is not above; it is a different dimension.

The thesis that some preachers are promoting, and I seriously believe that the devil is using to bring confusion, is: God has given the Church authority to cast out devils on the earth, but we have no power to fight in the heavenly places.

We can all definitely agree that the kingdom of darkness is well coordinated and structured. Demonic forces cooperate cohesively for their own survival. So now, let's imagine the following situation. Suppose a territorial power in the second heaven governs a region. It feels untouchable; since the Christians have no power against it. Meanwhile, its army gleefully casts down all sorts of terrible evil upon the earth. Then this power discovers that the Christians get excited because they have authority over its army, by binding and casting them out.

Do you really think this power of darkness is going to sit back, cross its arms, and allow this to happen? Not on your life. Many churches have failed to understand this fundamental issue. They began with great success but became complacent over time. These churches have been divided by conflict or have been destroyed by sin, having no idea how to defend themselves. What is their response to such attack? They respond by saying, "For the battle is God's, let Him fight for us." However, from God we also receive salvation. Do we say therefore: "You, oh Lord, preach to these towns." The one reaction is as senseless as the other.

In several areas of Scripture, it's mentioned that satan was cast out of heaven unto the earth. This doesn't mean he was cast out of the second heaven or heavenly realms and only has authority on the earth, it means his rights and position in God's Kingdom were removed.

One of these passages in Isaiah 14 and Ezekiel 28:11-19 recounts the fall of Lucifer, the Protective Cherubim. He was a servant among the hosts of God and was banished from his heavenly position in the third heaven.

"Thou hast defiled thy sanctuaries by the multitude of thine iniquities, by the iniquity of

thy traffick; therefore will I bring forth a fire
from the midst of thee, it shall devour thee, and
I will bring thee to ashes upon the earth in the
sight of all them that behold thee."

                                                    -Ezekiel 28:18

We know this occurred before the creation of Adam when all heavenly realms were already in existence and it is here that the devil has established his rule.

Revelation 12:9-11 is another fragment from the Word that speaks of the time when satan was banished from heaven, it says:

"And the great dragon was cast out, that old
serpent, called the Devil, and Satan, which
deceiveth the whole world: he was cast out into
the earth, and his angels were cast out with him.
And I heard a loud voice saying in heaven, Now
is come salvation, and strength, and the kingdom
*of our God, and the power of his Christ: **for the***
***accuser of our brethren is cast down,** which*
accused them before our God day and night. And
they overcame him by the blood of the Lamb, and
by the word of their testimony; and they loved
not their lives unto the death."

We read in this passage as well as in Ezekiel how satan lost his position in the third heaven. In his fall, before the world was created, he lost his position as director of heavenly worship. He lost his place as a "public prosecutor". It is like a businessman being thrown out of a company. Lucifer lost his position in God's heavenly kingdom, but he still moves in the spiritual world.

2.- Jesus destroyed the devil's entire empire and gave us all authority.

The victory at the cross was not partial. Jesus defeated satan and all his governmental structures. In His authority, Jesus did not only conquer demons that inhabit people but also demons that operate outside human bodies.

When Jesus was casting out devils here on earth, He had not yet at that time completely conquered the devil. But after His resurrection He said to his disciples: **"All power is given unto me in heaven and in earth" (Matthew 28:18b).** After this He gave them the great commission to go into the world and to establish the kingdom of God on earth.

Establishing God's kingdom implies entering territories that are terribly occupied by the forces of darkness. The power of God must first destroy the principalities ruling those territories so that the Gospel can advance successfully. If done in another way, the results will be very poor and, sometimes, devastating for those who try.

Jesus said:

> "*But if I cast out devils by the Spirit of God, then the kingdom of God is come unto you. Or else how can one enter into a strong man's house, and spoil his goods, except he first bind the strong man? and then he will spoil his house.*"
>
> -*Matthew 12:28-29*

For many years, Mexico, my country of origin, was one of the places with the highest number of martyrs on earth. The skies were of bronze, and there were occasions when the advancement of the kingdom caused the death of precious servants of God. Before I understood how to wage spiritual warfare, I saw many pastors fall into the most abominable sins. I saw churches destroyed and others swallowed up by freemasonry, while their pastors failed to realize what they were getting themselves into. Other churches had established themselves in areas governed by the powers of death; and there their people were persecuted by sickness, heart attacks, accidents or simply, spiritual death.

There were thousands of disheartened pastors everywhere. The churches became engaged in lifeless and religious routines, and slowly lost their members one by one. This is not only happening in Mexico but all over the world. The reason for this is clearly stated by Jesus: "We can't enter a strong man's house to rob him without first tying him up." We began to wage strategic spiritual warfare in Mexico in 1994, raising the army of God throughout the country. We saw radical changes in the nation. Churches emerged in a power and revival took place in many areas of the country.

The opening of the heavens was noticeable. A powerful movement of the Holy Spirit has entered the nation. God raised up men and women at national and international levels because we have come to understand our authority in Jesus Christ and we repossessed the land.

In the Old Testament, which is a shadow of what is to come in the New, God gave the Promised Land to Joshua. But it was a land occupied by giants, which he had to defeat. It is the same way in all the nations today. Our country is part of the inheritance given to us by God, but we have to cast out the territorial spirits occupying it.

> *"Ask of me, and I shall give thee the heathen for thine inheritance, and the uttermost parts of the earth for thy possession."*
>
> *-Psalms 2:8*

God has given us all authority in Christ because we are the Lord's own body. The body of Christ is as powerful as His head. Otherwise, we are not connected to the true authority.

Can the body say to the head: "I'm not fighting with these devils; you fight them alone"? Or, is it not the head the one that gives power to the body to execute all that it wants? May God enlighten the eyes of our understanding so that we may see His riches in glory! As it says in Scripture:

> *"And what is the exceeding greatness of his power to us-ward* **who believe,** *according to the working of his mighty power, which he wrought in Christ, when he raised him from the dead, and set him at his own right hand* **in the heavenly places, Far above all principality, and power, and might, and dominion,** *and every name that is named, not only in this world, but also in that which is to come: And hath put all things under his feet, and gave him to be the head over all things to the church,* **Which is his body, the fulness of him that filleth all in all."**   *-Ephesians 1:19-23*

If we are the fullness of Christ, how can we say He has all the authority and we only have a limited authority? The body and the head have the same power, if they are connected one to another.

Jesus is not separated from His Church, so to speak, sitting in His heavenly throne, leaving us with only a limited authority here on earth, and abandoning us to the mercy of the territorial spirits to do whatever they want. Jesus is in our midst. "For in Him we live and move and have our being." In Jesus, there is no division between heaven and earth. The Bible says:

> *"Having made known unto us the mystery of his will, according to his good pleasure which he hath purposed in himself: That in the dispensation of the fulness of times he might gather together in one all things in Christ, both which are in heaven, and which are on earth; even in him:"*
> *-Ephesians 1:9, 10*

In my opinion, it is a tremendous theological error to say that Jesus has all the authority in the heavens and that we only have authority here on earth. I insist that Jesus is not separated from His true saints.

> *"But he that is joined unto the Lord is one spirit."*
> *-1 Corinthians 6:17*

This is the intimate communion we have with the Spirit of the Lord.

> *"...as thou, Father, art in me, and I in thee, that they also may be one in us ..."*   *-John 17:21*

He who is united with Jesus, who is under His Lordship and sanctification, **is truly one with Jesus.** "One" does not mean that Jesus is above in the heavens and that we are here on earth. One means "one." Jesus said: **The kingdom of God is in the midst of us."** This means, within our spirits. The kingdom of God has in itself all of the authority of its King.

Jesus said to Peter, as an example of the apostolic authority of the Church:

> "And I say also unto thee, That thou art Peter, and upon this rock I will build my church; and the gates of hell shall not prevail against it. And I will give unto thee the keys of the kingdom of heaven: and whatsoever thou shalt bind on earth shall be bound in heaven: and whatsoever thou shalt loose on earth shall be loosed in heaven."
> -Matthew 16:18, 19

These keys refer to nothing else but to the authority of God, to affect the earth as well as the heaven. The gates of hell represent the government of the satanic empire, which has been overthrown by the Church.

Our Lord also said:

> "Behold, I give unto you power to tread on serpents and scorpions, and over all the power of the enemy: and nothing shall by any means hurt you."
> -Luke 10:19

This sentence refers to all kinds of serpents, more than just those that crawl. It refers to the ancient serpents (Genesis 3:14), the dragon serpent in Revelation 12:9, and the flying serpents in Isaiah 30: 6 and the water serpents Isaiah 27:1.

There are people who continue to see Leviathan, a terrible water serpent, as a monster nobody can approach much less destroy, as stated in the book of Job. The truth is, Jesus defeated every demon and monster from hell at the cross of Calvary. We can now tread on all serpents in the authority of Jesus. This is what the Lord said.

The truth is, when you experience the power of God in territorial warfare, the most terrible demons are like toys in comparison to the fearsome majesty and authority of our God. When we fight, (I am speaking to those whom God has called to the frontlines of battle, and I will speak more about this later on), we are not like tiny Roman toy soldiers, with a tiny little sword and shield as illustrated in Sunday school materials. We are extremely powerful in Him. The size of our spirit becomes gigantic when united with Jesus! We have armor, which is the same armor as God's. It is impenetrable and indestructible, full of flames of fire and sparks of power emitting from it.

> *"For the weapons of our warfare are not carnal, but mighty through God to the pulling down of strong holds."*   *-2 Corinthians 10:4*

God has invested His great power in us. Our comprehension of this will create great fear in the ranks of the devil. The Word says, demons believe and tremble before God. We are clothed in Him and our lives are hidden in Christ Jesus.

Some people consider the devil, the leviathan, and other territorial powers as if they have the greatest power. This is exactly what satan wants people to believe; to intimidate the army of God into leaving him alone to do as he wishes. With these beliefs, he can intimidate the army of God, and continue to damage and rule as he wants.

3. - The authority of angels and of the Church.
a) Misunderstood paragraphs.

I have read books wherein the authors say that the church does not have the power to rebuke satan. They based their theology on two passages, namely a passage in Jude, and the other one in Peter. We have already earlier established that God has given us all authority to tread upon serpents and scorpions, and that nothing will harm us.

To tread means to "place under our feet, step on them, and then crush them to pieces." These terms speak more forcefully than the word 'rebuke.' The word 'rebuke' in Greek is "epitimao," which means 'to admonish.' Besides this, it has also a legal connotation, meaning "to censure, restrict, or to bring charges against someone in a court of law." In his epistle, the apostle Jude warns against false teachers who emerge in the midst of the people of God. This letter is a warning against men who are full of iniquity, and who infiltrate the church. The apostle clearly shows how to identify these false teachers. But Jude's letter does not deal with the authority of true believers over satan. Observing the written context of this doctrine is important to maintain its validity. If we want to articulate and maintain sound doctrine, it is important to take the entire context of specific verses into account.

> *"For there are certain men crept in unawares, who were before of old ordained to this condemnation, ungodly men, turning the grace of our God into lasciviousness, and denying the only Lord God, and our Lord Jesus Christ."*
>
> *-Jude 1:4*

"Likewise also these filthy dreamers defile the flesh, despise dominion, and speak evil of dignities. Yet Michael, the archangel, when contending with the devil he disputed about the body of Moses, **durst not bring against him a railing accusation**, but said, The Lord rebuke thee." (This took place when Michael was arguing with Satan about Mose body). "But these speak evil of those things which they know not: but what they know naturally, as brute beasts, in those things they corrupt themselves."
-Jude 1: 8 – 10 (The notes from 2 Peter 2:9 – 22 are analogous to Jude).

It is very clear from the passage we just read that 'these people' is not a reference to the army of God on earth but to people who are not even Christians. The majority of us know this type of conceited people: They behave as if they are gods and make fun of the devil and his hosts; in reality they are atheists without any fear of God.

The question is: Does the born again Christian have authority to rebuke the devil? I believe the only one who can put satan under divine justice is God, the Triune God. But in His sovereignty, He delegates this authority, all the more because we are one in spirit with the Spirit of the Lord. It is Christ Jesus in us who rebukes the devil with all sober authority, and who places him under divine justice. Jesus sits at the right hand of the Father, waiting

"...till his enemies be made his footstool."
-Hebrews 10:13b

I believe it is part of the Holy Spirit's mission on earth to use the church to remind satan that he has been judged and defeated. This is what it means to 'rebuke.'

"And when he is come, he will reprove the world of sin, and of righteousness, and of judgment: Of sin, because they believe not on me; Of righteousness, because I go to my Father, and ye see me no more; Of judgment, because the prince of this world is judged." John 16:8-11

So, it is not the church that takes action in judging the devil independently from God. But it is the Holy Spirit in the believer, who reminds satan of what God has already done. It is not a matter of shouting at the devil, but of giving Jesus the legal right to place him under divine judgment through our prayers. The believer who truly has united his life to Jesus, has become His body, and has become larger than the angels.

> *"Who being the brightness of his glory, and the express image of his person, and upholding all things by the word of his power, when he had by himself purged our sins, sat down on the right hand of the Majesty on high; Being made so much better than the angels, as he hath by inheritance obtained a more excellent name than they."*
>
> *-Hebrews 1:3, 4*

We need to understand first of all, that believers are co-heirs with Christ, not apart from Christ. When the Word speaks about angels, we see clearly that the angels do not share with the believers the right to be co-heirs with Christ. "Aren't all ministering spirits sent to serve in favor of those who are heirs of salvation?" It is certainly true that Michael did not dare to speak judgment on the devil. The first reason was that satan had not been judged yet by the death of Christ. The second reason was that none of the angels are co-heirs with Christ nor are they part of His body. And thirdly, the total authority over the adversary, which Jesus has given to His church, He has not given to any of the angels.

b) The motive of this war is the compassion of Jesus.

Spiritual warfare is not just a new spiritual trend. Nor does the Spirit give us the option to choose whether to take part in it or not. God has called all of us to be His soldiers, though the level at which each of us is called varies from person to person. We are God's army on earth, which He uses to destroy the works of the enemy and to establish His kingdom.

On the other hand, the devil has also declared war. He roams like a roaring lion, seeking for someone to devour. He is killing, stealing and destroying wherever he can. And his armies are deployed to take the nations to the darkest, most violent and most infernal era in history. This produced terrible pain in the heart of God. The call to warfare is really central to the gospel. Because of God's great love, He rescued mankind from the destructive claws of the devil. That is why He gave up His most precious and beloved Son.

God rescued me from satan's terrible torments. Satan placed a heavy yoke, which pressed on me consistently day and night. I was without any hope, not even aware of the possibility that there was a way out. So, I simply accepted my fate and lived in profound suffering. I remember the time when I cried for 365 days. Those were days of darkness, fear and constant harassment from unexpected injustices and misfortunes; it was a time when these severe afflictions tore my soul apart.

The Word says:

> *"Have respect unto the covenant: for the dark places of the earth are full of the habitations of cruelty."* -Psalm 74:20

The devil is not only found in areas dominated by witches and warlocks. He fills the entire earth with aggression and violence. We find aggression and violence in the following: in homicides, in drunken husbands who beat their wives to death, in murderers who kill children in schools, in fathers who abuse their daughters sexually, in young people who die of overdoses of drugs, in thousands of people jailed because of lawlessness, and in people who live in inhuman poverty. Other people fall victim to incurable diseases expecting an idol of wood to save them. There are thousands of children who run away from home due to parental abuse and still others who are emotionally scarred due to abandonment. There are children found alone at the age of two or three, sometimes being looked after by an older sibling who is just five or six years old. They live in sewers, and become an easy prey to satanists who need them for sacrificial purposes and take them without anyone noticing. One time, two children sat in the street, one child was quietly hugging a little sister who was just killed by a hit and run driver. They were both quiet because the one holding the sister died also, by freezing to death. This is not an exaggeration; there are countries where children are killed like rats because their governments do not know what to do with them.

The Bible says:

"For we know that the whole creation groaneth and travaileth in pain together until now."
                                        -Romans 8:22

In the heart of every man, woman and child, exists an internal uproar, which is inaudible to us, but rings loudly in the heart of God. It is a heartrending scream, which at times can only be heard in the most profound intercession, and when heard, you cannot keep yourself from crying. God hears this every day and at all hours. God hears the cry of millions upon millions of embryos calling out to live and, nevertheless, assassinated.

Are you aware dear reader, the magnitude of the cries coming from wives and mothers who carry insufferable burdens? They are abandoned or left alone to care for the family while their husbands drown themselves in drink, arrive home covered in vomit, asking to have their carnal appetites satiated.

God allowed me to experience in a personal and varied way, what it's like to live amid the pain of human anguish as I go out to help others. I have pastored in zones of such darkness it is nearly impossible to describe the level of wickedness and oppression existing in these places. I have visited places where evil exists in such a dominant form that it tears the soul. You have to be made of wood to not discern the pain as you walk through the streets in India or Africa. You can literally see the corpses of those dead from famine lying in the streets. Children are nibbled on by rats as they live in places so unsanitary you can't breathe the malodorous air. As you walk by the entrance halls of the Hindu temples, rivers of blood from sacrificed animals spill over the patios while babies are offered to the powers of hell.

It is painful to see how the lives of women living in Muslim countries are destroyed. They have no life; they receive nothing and are treated worse then the animals while no one rescues them from the cruelty of their husbands. In places such as Haiti and in Buddhist countries, the people walk as if they're zombies; their souls are completely possessed by demons.

The kingdom of darkness is tremendously cruel and merciless. It never pardons anyone and destroys like an incessant drip or plague that never ends.

"If thou seest the oppression of the poor, and violent perverting of judgment and justice in a province, marvel not at the matter: for he that is

higher than the highest regardeth; and there be
higher than they."   *-Ecclesiastes 5:8*

Jesus listens to the pain of a tortured world, and it moves Him to the innermost fiber of His heart. By any chance, are we not aware how much and how profoundly God loves the world? Perhaps for some the revelation millions are going to hell doesn't move them because they live in all conceivable comfort, giving their offerings while others do the work. They're assured of their place in heaven and this gives them a sense of peace, but in God's heart, this isn't the case.

When the Word says Jesus bore our pain and suffering, it also means Father God feels the pain of every living being upon the earth. Man is whom God loves the most; He loves us so much He gave His only begotten Son to suffer the worst of our torment unto the death.

Dearest reader, please be aware of this. Each one of us who calls ourselves a human being; we are the most beloved of God. Every day God sees how those whom He loves are violated, outraged, murdered, and, tormented by unimaginable cruelty. All of this is before His eyes, day and night.

Imagine how you'd feel seeing the person you loved the most tortured right before you. This is how God feels every day as He sees the pain of the lost. Jesus is in heaven interceding on our behalf, looking for those who will join Him in unraveling the works of evil. Do you really think Jesus doesn't long for an army to rise up fully vested in His authority, motivated by profound compassion?

The Devil is stealing compassion away from the Church. Only a Church who understands the pain God feels and senses in their bones the suffering experienced by those oppressed by the devil, will rise to wage war, no matter what the cost.

I remember one occasion when I warred from the highest mountain in Peru against a powerful spilling of blood, which constantly flowed due to massacres. The Devil launched a violent attack against my physical heart. I felt I was dying. I couldn't walk ten steps without the sensation my heart would burst at any moment. I prayed with all the strength I know, until I reached a point I knew I couldn't take another step. I said to the Lord: "I don't know how to pray. What is the power I need to win?" At that moment, the mountain was filled with the glory of God and a mantel of light cascaded from the peak, which completely covered us. I heard the voice of God say in a tremendous resonant voice: "It's My love, daughter, My love is the greatest force in the entire universe. In love, you will accomplish things that cannot be done in any other way!" His glory filled the faces of the Peruvians and He said: "Look how I love them! Look how I love them!" My entire being filled with an indescribable love, an energy which instantly invigorated me. My heart was instantly healed. We climbed to the top of Huascarán, and history shows something huge was removed from the skies of Peru.

It's the love and compassion for those who are suffering from within, creating a heart that wants to wage warfare against all principalities and powers which drag millions to hell. If you don't feel the pain, if compassion doesn't inflame your soul, if our longing is to live happily content in a beautiful home with a car outside the door, we haven't understood the Evangelism of Jesus. If our prayers are directed only towards our own needs and those of our loved ones, and we live with the preoccupation the devil is going to do what he wants, we are still much in need of more light. If a book or teaching falls into our hands allowing the devil to intimidate us, making us abandon our posts as soldiers as we seek to save ourselves and all we value, we have not learned to love as Jesus loved.

> *"This is my commandment, That ye love one another, as I have loved you. Greater love hath no man than this, that a man lay down his life for his friends."*   *-John 15:12, 13*

Warfare carries risks, even more so when it is done out of order (we will discuss this in depth later), but God protects those who offer their lives for others.

"And they lifted up their voices, and said, Jesus,
Master, have mercy on us."   *-Luke 17:13*

The real love of Christ for lost souls has cost many missionaries and their families their lives, and yet they didn't stop praying. The great intercessor and orator who went to China, Hudson Taylor, lost his life on the mission field. Wesley lost his woman, who was invaded by demons that wanted to destroy him and his ministry.

Mary Woodworth-Etter lost four of her children in order to be used and raised up in the miraculous power God placed her in. How many children never saw their mom and dad again after they left for the mission field in Africa; whose parents who died from some terrible disease? The history of true Evangelism is full of martyrs, men and women who denied themselves unto death so the reign of God could be established.

As it says in the book of Revelation 12:11:

"And they overcame him by the blood of the
Lamb, and by the word of their testimony; and
they loved not their lives unto the death."

Confronting the darkness of their days cost Stephen, Peter and Santiago their lives including most of the other apostles and thousands of martyrs. I could fill books with the names of all the children of God who loved this fallen world more then their own lives and possessions and all that was dear to them.

Spiritual warfare is the outward expression of the compassionate heart of God who cannot rest while there is pain and evil in the world. This is what spurs us onward to battle and combat all types of powers.

I have declared in my country and to all nations where God allows me to enter to do battle, that the Devil and I can't occupy the same place at the same time. If God has given me a nation I won't leave any demon or gods unworried or undisturbed. I can't hear the cries of a desperate nation, the heart of God aching for His people, and not give my life unto death.

There is too much compassion and love in my heart for those who suffer to not go out and fight, to give my all for them. I know many will not succumb or be moved by the intimidation of the devil because they are the true army of God.

4

Different types of War

1. The cleansing of the Land

I n all the territories that we set ourselves to conquer we find that the land has been contaminated by the sins of men and consecrated to the enemy through diverse covenants. For this reason the first thing we have to do is purify it and cancel all the pacts that have been entered over it.

> *"Yea, in heart ye work wickedness; ye weigh the violence of your hands in the earth."*
>
> *-Psalm 58:2*

To do this, it is important to understand the history of the territory: the shedding of blood, the consecrations to pagan gods made by the different cultures, the corporate sins such as massacres, inquisition, abuse against the indigenous people or the minority population, sexual debauchery to give power to a governor of darkness, child sacrifice and things of the sort.

Everything that is currently being manifested in a city once had its inception in history. For example, places where the innocent were sacrificed in the past yield as a result a strong tendency to abortion. The occult and drug addiction abound in places where sorcery was once present. According to Hosea chapter 4, prostitution, adultery, and fornication come from idolatry.

> "My people ask counsel at their stocks, and their staff declareth unto them: for the spirit of whoredoms hath caused them to err, and they have gone a whoring from under their God. They sacrifice upon the tops of the mountains, and burn incense upon the hills, under oaks and poplars and elms, because the shadow thereof is good: therefore your daughters shall commit whoredom, and your spouses shall commit adultery. I will not punish your daughters when they commit whoredom, nor your spouses when they commit adultery: for themselves are separated with whores, and they sacrifice

with harlots: therefore the people that doth not understand shall fall."   -Hosea 4:12-14

The first thing we need to do is identifyingly confess the sins and the iniquity of our ancestors or of the inhabitants of the land. The prophet Daniel humbled himself in this manner identifying with the sins of the people and this brought as a result the deliverance of the people of Israel from their captivity in Babylon.

"In the first year of his reign I Daniel understood by books the number of the years, whereof the word of the LORD came to Jeremiah the prophet, that hewould accomplish seventy years in the desolations of Jerusalem. And I set my face unto the Lord God, to seek by prayer and supplications, with fasting, and sackcloth, and ashes: And I prayed unto the LORD my God, and made my confession, and said, O Lord, the great and dreadful God, keeping the covenant and mercy to them that love him, and to them that keep his commandments; We have sinned, and have committed iniquity, and have done wickedly, and have rebelled, even by departing from thy precepts and from thy judgments: Now therefore, O our God, hear the prayer of thy servant, and his supplications, and cause thy face to shine upon thy sanctuary that is desolate, for the Lord's sake."   Daniel 9:2-5, 9:17*

It is important to remember that every war has to be directed by the Holy Spirit. It is through his moaning that cannot be uttered and the tongues of the Spirit that we will pray, as we ought.

> *"Likewise the Spirit also helpeth our infirmities: for we know not what we should pray for as we ought: but the Spirit itself maketh intercession for us with groanings which cannot be uttered."*
>
> *Romans 8:26*

The biographers of the great Evangelist Charles Finney, recount how he would withdraw himself into the woods or to isolated places where he could be heard groaning like a bear for the salvation of a city. I learned this from him and many a time we withdrew ourselves to the woods to groan for a place until the Lord will turn His countenance and extend His favor upon the land.

When in 1989 I looked at Mexico, desolate, barely having any churches, governed by the queen of heaven and the yoke of an inquisitor clergy, I determined myself to do whatever it took to deliver it.

God spoke to me to gather 70 pastors and intercessors to pray dramatically. One evening we groaned during three hours non-stop, blood would come from our throats, we would fall faint and get up. The stronger ones would impart strength to the ones who would grow faint and then they would rise again. Nothing stopped us till we saw the bronze heavens part and the light begin to shine.

I know this night changed the history of my country and it was the beginning of a war that lasted seven years until revival was seen. We held many public repentance campaigns. At one of them in the central plaza, in the Zócalo in the City of Mexico, thousands of persons brought their idols and we broke them publicly asking God forgiveness for the idolatry of Mexico.

At many other cities we would gather a large amount of people in the plazas and they would publicly confess their sins and then those of the city. The authority to ask forgiveness for the sins of others comes when we dare confess our own. I will talk about this further on.

God sometimes performs signs and wonders to cleanse the land from sin. When we took over Hitler's concentration camps in Poland, something marvelous happened. It was the month of May, the dry season in that nation; the Lord gave us the instruction to penetrate the camp in Aushwitz-Birkenau at three in the morning. We stealthily infiltrated it through a forest until we ran into the crematory furnaces where more than 4 million died. The land was cursed and diabolically entered into covenant with by the acts of the occult of the German Führer. We groaned in the Spirit for a long time, asking forgiveness and crying out for the redemption of the German and Polish people. All of a sudden, Heaven began to literally roar, the blast of the thunderclap making even the bravest shudder. We were before the indignation itself of the Lion of Judah. All of a sudden there was a bursting explosion, the whole heavens crackled mightily and the tempest began out of nowhere. Torrents of water were loosed from Heaven and we heard the voice of the Most High saying: I am cleansing the land from the shedding of the blood. When the rain began to let up, the sun appeared in the horizon and a double rainbow extended from side to side above the concentration camp. A new day full of hope was dawning over Europe.

2. - Establishing the territory

Once the land is washed, borders have to be established since God gives out territories according to limits. This is part of the Law of Territories. When God gave the Promised Land to Israel, He determined its property and jurisdiction limits.

> *"Every place that the sole of your foot shall tread upon, that have I given unto you, as I said unto Moses.   From the wilderness and this Lebanon even unto the great river, the river Euphrates, all the land of the Hittites, and unto the great sea toward the going down of the sun, shall be your coast."*   *Joshua 1:3-4*

Once the land has been delimited, it has to be consecrated to Jehovah, The first thing Joshua did before taking possession of the Promised Land was to lift up an altar to the Lord.

> *"Take you twelve men out of the people, out of every tribe a man, And command ye them, saying, Take you hence out of the midst of Jordan, out of the place where the priests' feet stood firm, twelve stones, and ye shall carry them over with you, and leave them in the lodging place, where ye shall lodge this night."*   *-Joshua 4:2-3*

God gave this same principle to Jacob so He could establish His Presence over the land.

> *"And the land which I gave Abraham and Isaac, to thee I will give it, and to thy seed after thee will I give the land. And God went up from him in the place where he talked with him."*
>   *-Genesis 35:12-13*

God needs a territorial legal right to be able to hand out possession of the land. The establishing of altars is like the signing of a purchase and sales contract which certifies the transfer of ownership.

> *"An altar of earth thou shalt make unto me, and shalt sacrifice thereon thy burnt offerings, and*

thy peace offerings, thy sheep, and thine oxen: in all places where I record my name I will come unto thee, and I will bless thee."

-Exodus 20:24

In the Old Testament we see great men of God following this principle of erecting altars over the land, such as Noah, Moses, Abraham, Jeremiah, David and many others. The law of territorial ownership is not only valid spiritually but it is a well-known requisite in the natural. When you buy a property, it contains limits surrounding it and you have to sign the Sales and Purchase agreement to become the legitimate owner.

Remember that the enemy understands perfectly about territorial matters; this is why he established altars and pacts in each culture that would give him the legal right to establish his principalities and rulers.

"For according to the number of thy cities were thy gods, O Judah; and according to the number of the streets of Jerusalem have ye set up altars to that shameful thing, even altars to burn incense unto Baal." *-Jeremiah 11:13*

The shamans, the priests of each civilization have been in charge of making sacrifices in valleys, lagoons, rivers, mountains, etc... and putting up monuments that demarcate each of the governor's territory.

When we put up an altar to God or various altars according to the direction of the Holy Spirit, we are sealing the land with a covenant greater than any the devil can do. Sometimes God gives us the instruction to set up anointed stakes in various key points of the city, as may be the case of its gates. Other times the Lord sends us to put up Bibles and twelve-stone altars.

Our ministry produces the smallest bibles in the world. The compete 66 books are in a transparent microfilm 2 by 3 cm and we make anointed tiny twelve-stone altars, prayed-for in minuscule little bags. We place these alongside the Bibles in strategic places where something big could never be placed.

We have also delimited territories by setting white painted stones with Bible verses in innumerable quantities around a city.

When we took over the Headwaters of the Rhine River in Switzerland we put a lambs' fleece sprayed with oil and the elements of the Lord's Supper symbolizing Jesus becoming enthroned on the Alps. On Mount Everest we put up a banner with all the names of God alongside a menorah and a replica of the Ark of the Covenant and a rod, symbolizing that of Aaron's. Everywhere that we take back territory, God instructs us on how He wants to delimit it.

This is not a matter of formulas, but of hearing the Holy Spirit.

In my book, "Shaking Heavens" I give a detailed explanation on the War Symbols, their meaning and their correct use. I also talk about strategies and the different weapons of war. Reading it will be a great blessing to you.

Whenever possible, it is important to surround the territory, anointing it and consecrating it to Jehovah, with prayer, worship and spiritual warfare caravans.

3. - Strategic Wars at the Prophetic Act Level

The next level is the Prophetic Acts. As its name indicates, these are acts that loose the power of the Kingdom of God upon a place. They are also used to confront the powers of darkness and bring judgment upon them.

Some examples of prophetic acts in the Bible are:

a) Joshua circling Jericho:
"And the LORD said unto Joshua, See, I have given into thine hand Jericho, and the king thereof, and the mighty men of valour. And ye shall compass the city, all ye men of war, and go round about the city once. Thus shalt thou do six

days. And seven priests shall bear before the ark seven trumpets of rams' horns: and the seventh day ye shall compass the city seven times, and the priests shall blow with the trumpets. And it shall come to pass, that when they make a long blast with the ram's horn, and when ye hear the sound of the trumpet, all the people shall shout with a great shout; and the wall of the city shall fall down flat, and the people shall ascend up every man straight before him."

-Joshua 6:2-5

b) Gideon using torches and clay vessels:

"And he divided the three hundred men into three companies, and he put a trumpet in every man's hand, with empty pitchers, and lamps within the pitchers. And he said unto them, Look on me, and do likewise: and, behold, when I come to the outside of the camp, it shall be that, as I do, so shall ye do. When I blow with a trumpet, I and all that are with me, then blow ye the trumpets also on every side of all the camp, and say, The sword of the LORD, and of Gideon."   *Judges 7:16-18*

c) Jeremiah is told to put stones inside the brickwork of Pharaoh's house:

"Take great stones in thine hand, and hide them

in the clay in the brickkiln, which is at the entry of Pharaoh's house in Tahpanhes, in the sight of the men of Judah; And say unto them, Thus saith the LORD of hosts, the God of Israel; Behold, I will send and take Nebuchadrezzar the king of Babylon, my servant, and will set his throne upon these stones that I have hid; and he shall spread his royal pavilion over them."

Jeremiah 43:9-10

d) Isaiah prophesying that a banner has to be put up in the high mountain:

"Lift ye up a banner upon the high mountain, exalt the voice unto them, shake the hand, that they may go into the gates of the nobles. I have commanded my sanctified ones, I have also called my mighty ones for mine anger, even them that rejoice in my highness."   *Isaiah 13:2-3*

We see examples such as these throughout the whole Bible, however they are not formulas but instructions that have to come from God indicating how He wants to wage war and what are the prophetic acts that have to be used.

At this level only proven prophets, and pastoral and prophetic intercession ministries should participate; people who qualify at a level of authority and demonic confrontation.   Josiah physically destroyed the altars on the high places so God could bring His Presence to the land, but he had the authority and the orders from Jehovah to do so. All his reform is narrated in Chapter 23 in the Book of Kings.

> *"He took the Asherah pole from the temple of the LORD to the Kidron Valley outside Jerusalem and burned it there. He ground it to powder and scattered the dust over the graves of the common people. He also tore down the quarters of the male shrine prostitutes that were in the temple of the Lord, the quarters where women did weaving for Asherah."*   *-2 Kings 23:6-7 (NKJV)*

In this type of war, God can give the order to anoint a territory by waging war from small airplanes and helicopters, or to enter dangerous places taken by satanists. The Lord will instruct how to take the mountains or the devil's government high places as well as the gates of hell, or how to go down to the caves at the bottom of the ocean. In 2009, God led us to wage a submarine war and for the first time a team of 16 high level scuba diver warriors went down to one of the corners of the Bermuda triangle. An extremely powerful door to the abyss, which was affecting a large part of the American continent, was found there and the Lord showed us how to topple it.

It's important to hear the instructions of the Holy Spirit and not to act following the example of somebody who wrote it in a book. For this type of confrontation we have to consider, the how, the when, the where, and the who. The times to act are decisive and the clear spiritual study of a territory is essential.

This is where I have found that there are more war setbacks and misfortunes since it is not taken into account that the majority of the territories do not operate isolated. The powers and principalities of darkness have organized communication lines and reinforcement stations.

> *"Art thou better than populous No, that was situate among the rivers, that had the waters round about it, whose rampart was the sea and her wall was from the sea? Ethiopia and Egypt were her strength, and it was infinite; Put and Lubim were thy helpers."*
>
> *-Nahum 3:8-9*

In this type of war, it is important to have rear guard prophetic intercessors who can take charge of unexpected attacks or enemy ambushes. This type of army will be able to discern the ruses of the enemy to protect the warriors in the front lines.

Not all wars require a frontal confrontation with the enemy. To besiege a fortified city and sever its water supply and provision ends up in a better strategy. This is the manner Persia conquered Babylon. They laid siege over it and diverted the river that supplied water to the city, he then made his armies penetrate the riverbed and thus he took the city. A spiritual stronghold replenishes itself from the shedding of blood, fornications and sexual abominations. Blood and illicit sex are the two fountains of life that the devil uses to strengthen himself. These are like rivers of iniquity that support it and have to be cut off.

Another provision that has to be cut off is the finances that aid the structures of evil.

A stronghold has demonic, heavenly, earthly, and maritime supply avenues through the underworld. These have to be cut off and dried out before entering the fray.

4. - Wars in the Dimension of the Spirit

This type of war is totally prophetic and in the spheres of the Spirit. It is the most efficient and secure way to organize an attack.

To carry it out, very seasoned warriors are required: people who can see in the spiritual world and know how the structures of darkness are organized over a city.

When we wage a war to deliver a territory we lead warriors to this level. We also invite pastors and intercessors who are evolving and who at least have some experience at the prophetic acts strategic warfare level.

We then form a central group not greater than twelve warriors, and we put the rest around ours. The only ones who have the freedom to speak what they hear and see in the spiritual world are the twelve. The rest form a support barrier and usually God includes the majority of them into seeing and hearing everything that is happening.

We then pray to God and enter the Spirit so the Lord can reveal to us how the invisible world is organized over a city or region that we have been sent to liberate.

Jesus said:

"Then answered Jesus and said unto them, Verily, verily, I say unto you, The Son can do nothing of himself, but what he seeth the Father do: for what things soever he doeth, these also doeth the Son likewise." -John 5:19

This is one of the most important principles in the Kingdom of God: to do nothing unless we first see The Father doing it. Jesus sent us out in the same power by which He was sent by The Father.

"As thou hast sent me into the world, even so have I also sent them into the world." -John 17:18

To have this, we need to be filled with the Holy Spirit, be trained in the gift of prophecy and in the knowledge of the spiritual realm.

The prophetic is not only saying; thus saith the Lord, but going deeply into the Kingdom of God and into His Wisdom. The Word says that the testimony of Jesus is the Spirit of Prophesy. (Revelations 19:10) This is told to John by the angel when he finds himself immersed in the heavenly regions, making him understand that everything he saw and heard in that realm was being testified and revealed by Jesus.

It is in that atmosphere of the Spirit that John sees the structures of the Great Babylon and its sentence, likewise those of the beast and of the false prophet.

We enter into this level of warfare following the model in which the Book of Revelation is developed. First John entered the Spirit and there he heard and saw the spiritual world.

> *"I was in the Spirit on the Lord's day, and heard*
> *behind me a great voice, as of a trumpet."*
> *-Revelation 1:10*

Second: he was taken into a deeper dimension after going through a door in Heaven where he presented himself before the throne of God to see and hear the things that were about to happen.

Third: God shows him how Heaven operates and how the judgments and the sentences from the Most High are executed. In our case, God has to grant us this level of warfare, the Blood of the Lamb has already opened the way into the Heaven and to the Throne of God at the moment the temple veil was torn.

God is raising warriors who have access and authority in these spheres. This is where God shows us all the structures of darkness and gives us instructions on how to confront them. Angels are assigned to us to fight alongside and weapons are assigned to us.   Therefore the battle is extremely powerful.

"The noise of a multitude in the mountains, like as of a great people; a tumultuous noise of the kingdoms of nations gathered together: the LORD of hosts mustereth the host of the battle. They come from a far country, from the end of heaven, even the LORD, and the weapons of his indignation, to destroy the whole land."
-Isaiah 13:4-5

Further ahead in this book we will see the interaction of the angels in the war of the saints.

Once the battle is fought in the spiritual world, we carry out on Earth the prophetic actions we saw in the Spirit. As we do this we are uniting Heaven and Earth and establishing what happened in the invisible world over the visible one.

The blessing in this type of warfare is that when we then carry out the prophetic acts and declarations in the territory, the powers of the spiritual world are already defeated and we thus avoid any counter-attack.

In Chapter One, I mentioned the war we waged in Uganda against one of the most feared warlocks of Africa. The success of that battle was due to how first we fought in the spiritual world against all the ancestral spirits that would aid the warlock. It was a marvelous battle where the angels took captive all of those spirits. We did this inside a house at the foothills of the mountain where the sorcerer dwelt.

Afterwards, when we went up to confront the warlock, the effects of what we had done could be seen. The man was furious; he would throw all sorts of death powders and bewitchment at us. He would yell at the top of his lungs to his ancestral spirits so that they would arrest us and not leave us until all evil should befall us. To his surprise, they were not responding despite the many magical arts and spells because the angels had already taken them away.

Desperate, due to his lack of power to hurt us, he called the police. When the officers arrived, a sizeable amount of the townspeople went up the mount to see what was happening, something which the Lord utilized in favor of His Kingdom.

The fire of the Spirit was upon us, and angels with flaming swords surrounded the shaman's cabin. Upon his seeing the angels, he ran to the police accusing us of wanting to burn his house down and they branded him as being insane and had him shut up.

Emboldened by everything that was happening, the pastor then took the word and boldly preached the gospel to all who had gathered. Half of the townspeople fell silent to the ground turning their lives over to Jesus Christ. Glory to God!

This war could've had another result, if it had not been fought correctly in the spiritual world. My sister forms part of the great cloud of witnesses of which the Book of Hebrews talks about. (Chapter 12:1)

The Body of Christ is active in Heaven. When John sees the martyrs in the Book of Revelation, he does not see them asleep or dead; they are alive crying out for justice.

"And when he had opened the fifth seal, I saw under the altar the souls of them that were slain for the word of God, and for the testimony which they held: And they cried with a loud voice, saying, How long, O Lord, holy and true, dost

thou not judge and avenge our blood on them that dwell on the earth?"   *-Revelation 6:9-10*

Jesus said:

"And as touching the dead, that they rise: have ye not read in the book of Moses, how in the bush God spake unto him, saying, I am the God of Abraham, and the God of Isaac, and the God of Jacob? He is not the God of the dead, but the God of the living: ye therefore do greatly err."

Mark 12:26-27

5

Who are called to do Warfare?

"And the LORD said unto Gideon, The people are yet too many; bring them down unto the water, and I will try them for thee there: and it shall be, that of whom I say unto thee, This shall go with thee, the same shall go with thee; and of whomsoever I say unto thee, This shall not go with thee, the same shall not go."   -Judges 7:4

1.- An Army Chosen by God

A lthough all of us are in the army of God and we all have a part in the battle, not all of us are called to fight in the front lines against principalities and territorial jurisdictions. God has chosen from among His people those He specifically wants to use for the liberation of nations and placed upon them a special anointing to wage particular warfare, gaining victory at these elevated levels.

In the Old Testament God is shown as a military God. One of the names given to Him is "Lord of Hosts." After observing and reading how Jehovah intervened to save His chosen people so many times through battle, we understand how He continues functioning in this capacity.

Each time God ordered warfare, He always chose someone on whom to place the victorious anointing of the Most High. The best example is King David.

From his youth God placed a powerful anointing for combat upon David. Not all have this anointing. When David fought against Goliath, the rest of the army of Israel was in confusion and subject to what the Philistines and the giant wanted to do to them. In this example, God used only one man to change the destiny of Israel. Anyone else who attempted to challenge the giant would have died, but God is the movement behind those who are chosen.

Much later, this same anointing fell upon David's army of valiant men. These men were at first battle weary and on the run, hidden in a cave named Adulam. However, when they saw the anointing that flowed from their commander, they were reenergized and transformed into mighty men of war. Pain creates revolutionaries!

Today, God still has His generals of war, united and called to liberate cities and countries. They're under a genuine covering, with lives that have been tested in great fires, able to transmit their anointing and lead armies in victory. Unfortunately, there are those who, acting on impulse with a true desire to see their cities liberated, launch wars without a calling or an anointing to do so by God. What subsequently occurs upon those who lead into battle and those who follow them are accidents and misfortunes. Even worse, these errors become the weapon the devil uses to intimidate the army of God.

Spiritual warfare is not a subject to go into or take lightly; it is a battle against an astute, tricky, and very real enemy. It requires preparation and very strict rules. To enter this kind of warfare with just enthusiasm and no real understanding, without a call from the Most High and without the necessary anointing, there's little doubt, very serious consequences will be experienced.

An experience that can shine light on this subject will be used as an analogy. God calls Gideon to go and wage war.

The first thing we encounter in telling this story is in regards to the people of Israel devastated by Midian. Israel's bounty has been robbed and great anguish is upon the people. They call out to God and God manifests Himself to one person, Gideon. God calls him, giving him the authority to win. It is still God who decides who will lead and be in His army.

> "And there came an angel of the LORD, and sat under an oak, which was in Ophrah, that pertained unto Joash the Abiezrite: and his son Gideon threshed wheat by the winepress, to hide it from the Midianites. And the angel of the LORD appeared unto him, and said unto him, The LORD is with thee, thou mighty man of valour."
>
> -Judges 6:11, 12

Gideon gathered the entire army of Israel but God said:

> "And the LORD said unto Gideon, The people that are with thee are too many for me to give the Midianites into their hands, lest Israel vaunt themselves against me, saying, Mine own hand hath saved me. Now therefore go to, proclaim in the ears of the people, saying, Whosoever is fearful and afraid, let him return and depart early from mount Gilead. And there returned of the people twenty and two thousand; and there remained ten thousand. And the LORD said unto

Gideon, The people are yet too many; bring them down unto the water, and I will try them for thee there: and it shall be, that of whom I say unto thee, This shall go with thee, the same shall go with thee; and of whomsoever I say unto thee, This shall not go with thee, the same shall not go. So he brought down the people unto the water: and the LORD said unto Gideon, Every one that lappeth of the water with his tongue, as a dog lappeth, him shalt thou set by himself; likewise every one that boweth down upon his knees to drink. And the number of them that lapped, putting their hand to their mouth, were three hundred men: but all the rest of the people bowed down upon their knees to drink water."

-Judges 7:2-6

Here we see how God selected His army. The three hundred were men who were alert, they carried the water to their mouths but their eyes were intent on all that was going on around them. This showed they were intelligent soldiers, easy to direct. Those who put their mouth in the stream, taking no precaution, symbolize those who do things any which way; they want to go to war, but don't take the time to learn the basic requirements. These will go in faith, but not with the total direction of the Holy Spirit.

Today we have magnificent authors who have written

about spiritual warfare with maps and battle strategies among other information. This however, is not much more than a support; they shine more light on a subject God has already spoken into the heart of the real warrior.

Problems arise when the experiences of others are studied and used as an operating manual, creating strategic formulas, which were fashioned only for a specific place with its own particular conditions and certain demons assigned only to that particular war. Reading books and speculating about warfare doesn't mean someone is ready to confront an enemy who has built itself enormous strength for that particular battle.

2.- Who cannot participate in the war?

"And the officers shall speak further unto the people, and they shall say, What man is there that is fearful and fainthearted? let him go and return unto his house, lest his brethren' heart faint as well as his heart."

-Deuteronomy 20:8

It's a mistake to involve immature and frightened people in a battle, having no clear understanding of the greatness of God over the devil; people whose souls need healing or in many cases, liberation. These people, because of their unresolved fears, become easy targets for the devil. Right now, I'm placing my focus on Divine selection, further ahead in the book I'll mention other important factors on who should not participate in the battle.

3.- Who qualifies for high level warfare?
a) Prophetic and Apostolic Authority

Spiritual warfare belongs specifically to the prophetic and apostolic sphere. Each ministry has a level of anointing and authority giving them the divine ability to function in what God has called them to do.

All are called and anointed, but not all are given the same function or purpose. To confuse the active limits of a ministry will bring consequences that will affect the body of Christ in a general and irremediable way.

For example, when a prophet is also a Pastor of a Church, and has no Pastoral ministry, the Church receives God's word but it is generally cut up, very profound, and possibly even confrontational. This will cause the faithful to receive little help with what they need; particularly in the problems they are experiencing. When an Evangelist wants to function as a Pastor he will, in general, have a huge motivation to Evangelize with manifestations of power, but in most cases, will have little profound revelation in the Word. The same thing occurs when Pastors, Teachers and Evangelists, want to pierce the areas of prophetic or apostolic authority. In general, what they will receive is confusion, unclear directions, and the problems will be the final result. Who, then, should be allowed to move in the spiritual world? It should be only those ministers who can discern the powers of darkness and the strategies to defeat them. Only prophets or other ministers with a prophetic anointing, such as pastor-prophets, teacher-prophets, apostle-prophets, can accomplish this in the correct way, like the apostles.

Any army must have authority and order. This is a crucial rule that cannot be changed, just as in natural warfare. Wouldn't it be highly dangerous for a captain in the United States Army to make decisions to bomb Iraq by himself? Of course it would.

We must do spiritual warfare against territorial powers like any other military organization. We must use clear-cut strategies, adequate weapons, and be in harmony and perfect order, from the generals down to the infantry.

b) Heavenly Selection

The Bible says in Proverbs 24:6:

> *"For by wise counsel thou shalt make thy war: and in multitude of counselors there is safety."*

In 1999, God showed me a vision that shook me with horror. I saw the devastating strength of the kingdom of darkness. It contained well-organized armies; their generals successfully coordinated their front troops, perfectly stationing them all over the world. They all fought for the same thing. Their principalities and rulers were perfectly united and structured in order to carry out satan's plans at the highest political, economic and religious levels over the entire face of the earth.

Impressive hierarchies of darkness were positioned in the form of secret societies, which governed not only in the visible realm but also protected diabolical plans. The plans were hidden by subterranean powers, which made them undetectable on the surface, therefore making them almost indestructible.

They had networks of provision and supplies as they fortified themselves in all parts of the world. Millions of demons went out over all the earth to incite people to sin and shed blood which made the walls of their fortresses even stronger and harder to overcome. They controlled the riches of some of the most powerful people on the planet.

I saw armies obey as they were sent to destroy churches and to eliminate the ministers of God. The people who were attacked the most were those who were alone. I saw these armies entering the churches with hardly any opposition as these spirits of arrogance, independence, gossip; division, sexual uncleanness, greed and power infected the people. I saw the church as tiny little lights dispersed throughout the nations, wanting to fight against a highly macabre and well-organized government.

As my heart became sorrowful with the vision, God comforted my soul and told me "let not your heart faint before the vision because the time has come in which I will manifest my government over the Earth. I have joined Heaven and Earth and I am choosing those who will rule by my side." While He was speaking to me, as lightning to my spirit came the word that says:

> *"These shall make war with the Lamb, and the Lamb shall overcome them: for he is Lord of lords, and King of kings:* **and they that are with him are called, and chosen, and faithful."**
> *-Revelation 17:14*

We see here that not everybody is meant to fight battles against demonic hierarchies on the side of the Lamb. God has chosen His army based on their faithfulness to Him. These people are faithful even at the most profound levels of the cross: self-denial and courage.

These are people who will walk in obedience even if the consequences would not be in their favor. The soldiers of God have a main priority; they follow God even if it costs them their lives. These are the ones who have the power to fight satan himself.

"And they overcame him by the blood of the Lamb, and by the word of their testimony; and they loved not their lives unto the death."

-Revelation 12:11

There is a degree of obedience to God which all of us can have. This pertains to keeping His commandments in our Christian activities and walk. However there are higher levels of obedience, which will determine whether we will be selected by God for His Highest purposes or eliminated from them.

Warfare in the heavenly realms requires warriors to have no fear; effective soldiers whom God can lead with just a simple look. These people are like the wind. God only has to breathe on them and they go where He sends them, because nothing ties them to this world. It is not primarily their valor and boldness that qualifies them, but the extent of dying to self. There are divine orders that mark the difference between those who will follow and those who will stay behind.

I remember the questions God asked me when He gave me the mission to climb Mount Everest, the highest summit on earth. The first question was: "How much do you long for the liberation of the 10/40 window if I do not guarantee that you will return alive? Will you still go?" (The 10/40 window consists of nations that were the least liberated or evangelized zones in the world in the 1990s.)

Few people know what it's like to say goodbye to their children while they ask you: "Mommy, God says you'll return, isn't this true?" Yet deep within you know the answer. Another question God asked me was: "What if I ask you to pay the great price of taking one of your most beloved, to liberate the fortress over Everest?" Nothing is more frightening than to see the life of a loved one and millions of souls dragged into hell hanging on a balance; the life of your beloved on one side of the balance and those numerous souls on the other.

The third question God asked was: "Are you willing to go to jail in Nepal so I can break the chains of its captives?" This question was by far the easiest one. All these three scenarios were about to happen. However, God changed his decree when I answered "Yes" and obeyed in everything, like God released Abraham from killing his son even though He had asked Abraham to sacrifice him.

God must test us before he can choose us, because we must overcome all levels of fear, confusion and pain in us before we can do battle.

c) Warriors of light

The ones that are chosen are warriors who have been trained in the light, for only the light of God can make the darkness disappear. The Word says:

"For the weapons of our warfare are not carnal,
but mighty through God to the pulling down of
strong holds;"   *-2 Corinthians 10:4*

It also says:

"let us therefore cast off the works of darkness,
and let us put on the armour of light."
                         –Romans 13:12b (NKJV)

The Light is the most powerful weapon that exists and no demon can resist it. The light is God Himself. In warfare we do not merely consider ourselves as people of light theologically, but we act as true torches producing the light of the Most High.

The real conflict is the confrontation between light and darkness. As the Apostle John said:

"In him was life; and the life was the light of
men. And the light shineth in darkness; and the
darkness comprehended it not."
                              -John 1:4, 5

According to a biblical principle darkness dissolves before the light. I don't have to scream for three hours for the darkness to leave every time I turn on a lamp at home. **The moment light manifests,** darkness disappears automatically. But if Jesus is the light that dwells within us, why does the darkness not disappear immediately all around us? The answer is that the light is still covered by real and substantial structures that the devil has built around men. These veils of darkness act like a solid blinder around a center that is full of light. The light exists, it is real, it dwells in the believer, but the fortresses of wickedness veil it. (My book "Iniquity" clearly speaks about this subject).

The presence of the light in the life of those who are called the children of God is one thing. But its visible manifestation through the lifestyle of the believer is quite another thing. There's an important difference between the presence of divine virtues in us and their full manifestation in us. A newly born again Christian immediately has, through faith, the presence of divine virtues and power, but these will not manifest in him immediately. These virtues and power only become visible after his old self is broken down and when he has gained understanding of the principles of the manifestation of light and of the kingdom of God.

The cross produces light since it is the death of Jesus that releases the power to conquer the devil. Satan knows that this is the only weapon he cannot fight against. The kingdom of darkness can distinguish those who are truly nailed to the cross and those who only talk about the cross.

The function of the light is to expose all things and

make them visible to others. On the cross Jesus brought all of our sins into the light. He not only died for all mankind, He also did it in a very public way. He counted Himself among the sinners. His nakedness that was exposed on the cross of Calvary represents the public exposure of all our transgressions. For this reason, those who come to the light do so as Jesus did, by exposing themselves through the confession of their sins.

There are sins of ignorance and certain attitudes, which we can confess to our Heavenly Father, but we must repent for and confess sins that we have consciously committed. The Bible says:

> *"Confess your faults one to another, and pray one for another, that ye may be healed. The effectual fervent prayer of a righteous man availeth much."*　　　　　　　　*-James 5:16*

Hardly anyone confesses sins in the present day churches. But it is biblical and will lead us into profound levels of light. The word to confess means to express one's sins in a public manner.

It's the same word we use when we say:

> *"For with the heart man believeth unto righteousness; and with the mouth confession is made unto salvation."*　　　　　*-Romans 10:10*

We know this does not mean to go to your room and to secretly tell the Lord that He is your Savior. Let's see what Scripture says:

> *"This then is the message which we have heard of him, and declare unto you, that God is light, and in him is no darkness at all. If we say that we have fellowship with him, and walk in darkness, we lie, and do not the truth: But if we walk in the light, as he is in the light, we have fellowship one with another, and the blood of Jesus Christ his Son cleanseth us from all sin."*   1 John 1:5-7

Take notice that the consequence of walking in the light is that we have communion with one another. It is incredible that the church claims that it is in the light, while communion with one another is what church members demonstrate the least. If people do not confess their sins and bring them into light, then they walk in concealment of the light, or, in other words, they walk in darkness. This kind of spiritual condition is the reason why we lose our power to fight against the devil. When we walk in such concealment, we move in the territory of the enemy where he has all the authority to attack us.

To expose sins is to walk in the light. It is a manifestation of great humility. It means entering into the reality of the cross completely naked, just like the Lord Jesus. The truth is that when everyone knows your sins, then the devil will no longer have any weapons to fight against you.

Confessing your sins with a sincere and contrite heart is painful but liberating at the same time. It will lead you into true repentance. You will never want to commit the same transgression again.

One of the Holy Spirit's functions is to remit the confessed sin. The church has also ceased doing that. This is extremely important in spiritual warfare because we cannot enter the dark regions of the enemy unless we have received remission for our sins.

> *"Whose soever sins ye remit, they are remitted unto them; and whose soever sins ye retain, they are retained."*   *-John 20:23*

This is perhaps the major problem that has caused damages in the camp of God when engaging in battle. To go out and fight without the confession and remittance of sin makes us easy targets of the enemy. It is the same as going on mission at night with a flashlight and megaphone to expose your position.

My warfare team and I have fought many mighty battles against great powers of darkness in the second heaven. One of the things we always do is to spend several days in a place completely cut off from the world, confessing all our sins, including attitudes, thoughts and dreams. We understand this part is vital in battle and that it gives us powerful protection from God.

The level of our confession determines the level at which we expose ourselves, and the level at which we expose ourselves determines the level at which light shines through us. God requires us to give our confession before a Holy Spirit filled believer who submits this confession to God, in order for Him to pardon and cleanse us from our transgressions. Nevertheless, there is tremendous power in the level at which we humiliate ourselves and the level at which we expose ourselves to others.

A public confession before the congregation demonstrates an impressive level of the cross. This of course is the prerogative of each of us. But those who die to their flesh in total humility will receive from God a large reward and attain a powerful level of light in the battle against evil.

This is one of the acts of high level obedience that God has asked from me. Over three consecutive years He asked me to confess my sins and failures before each assembly I was invited to around the world. Wherever the devil tried to attack me, he was immediately disarmed. It was horrible. I suffered so much every time I had to do it, especially in places that were full of religiosity and legalism. However, every time I did this, I saw satan fall like lightning.

When I entered into battle before, and even today, the light of God shines in my life from the distance, and I can see demons fall like birds hit by lightning. To God be all the glory!

We have conducted crusades of public repentance of sin and we have heard the skies literally roar with supernatural thunder as the pastors and people humbled themselves and confessed their sins. How easy it becomes to fight when an entire village is literally immersed in His blood and forgiveness. Hallelujah!

d) The heavens fight alongside the chosen ones.

God has two types of armies, the heavenly and the earthly ones. Both types of armies interact when our Lord calls us to battle.

In many sections of the Bible we see them working together. For Elisha this was so obvious that he stayed in perfect peace even when surrounded by his enemies, knowing he was very well protected in the midst of their aggression.

> *"Therefore sent he thither horses, and chariots, and a great host: and they came by night, and compassed the city about and when the servant of the man of God was risen early, and gone forth, behold, an host compassed the city both*

*with horses and chariots. And his servant said
unto him, Alas, my master! how shall we do? And
he answered, Fear not: for they that be with us
are more than they that be with them. And Elisha
prayed, and said, LORD, I pray thee, open his
eyes, that he may see. And the LORD opened the
eyes of the young man; and he saw: and, behold,
the mountain was full of horses and chariots of
fire round about Elisha."*   *-2 Kings 6:14-17*

Another great passage speaks of the judgment of mount
Babylon:

*"I have commanded my sanctified ones; I have
also called my mighty ones for mine anger, even
them that rejoice in my highness. The noise of
a multitude in the mountains, like as of a great
people; a tumultuous noise of the kingdoms of
nations gathered together: the LORD of hosts
mustereth the host of the battle. 5 They come
from a far country, from the end of heaven, even
the LORD, and the weapons of his indignation, to
destroy the whole land."*   *-Isaiah 13:3-5*

Once again, we see that God chooses as His instruments
people who are brave and consecrated to war. What we
have read does not speak of just any battle. It speaks of
combat at a very high level, which affects the entire world.

When confronting high level demonic principalities, God always sends His heavenly troops to carry out the most difficult part of the fight. In most battles the Lord allows us to face danger up to a certain point, and then by His grace He sends His angels to do what we cannot accomplish. When an earthly warrior has ascended sufficiently in rank, God will give him on some occasions the great honor to fight the devil face to face with the assistance of the angels.

Only God can grant such privilege, and there are very few people on earth who have received it. In order to receive such a marvelous assignment from our Lord, you need to win many battles and to acquire experience and courage through the Holy Spirit.

In Revelation 12:7-10, God shows us a battle in which we clearly see the interaction between the two types of armies develop.

> *"And there was war in heaven: Michael and his angels fought against the dragon; and the dragon fought and his angels, and prevailed not; neither was their place found any more in heaven. And the great dragon was cast out, that old serpent, called the Devil, and Satan, which deceiveth the whole world: he was cast out into the earth, and his angels were cast out with him. And I heard a loud voice saying in heaven, 'Now is come salvation, and strength, and the kingdom of our*

God, and the power of his Christ: for the accuser
of our brethren is cast down, which accused them
before our God day and night."

Notice that the same heavenly voice declares who are
the ones who have defeated him. It does not say Michael
and his angels have defeated him. This is what it says:

"And they overcame him by the blood of the
Lamb, and by the word of their testimony; and
they loved not their lives unto the death."

-Revelation 12:11

They are obviously the chosen saints of God.

The voice in Heaven declares the devil as being defeated
and the warriors announce it over the Earth. Some think
that the children of God cannot personally confront the
devil and wage war against him here on earth and much
less in the heavens. Yet we see in this great battle that the
winners are precisely the children of the Most High.

The voice declared that the devil has been defeated in
this battle. Nevertheless he continues to act against the
church on earth (as the rest of this chapter shows.) The
powers of darkness have been overthrown and cast down
from heaven but this does not imply that they have been
annihilated completely. However, it is clear that their
removal from the heavenly regions has robbed them of

their main operational strength as God has declared them defeated.

e) Our weapons are powerful in God

Spiritual warfare is from the Spirit. The anointing to wage war and to receive God's grace for victory is the result of a life that is filled with God.

Nevertheless there are people who love to do warfare but who totally ignore the basic laws of personal protection and the understanding that is necessary to fight the war. This has serious consequences. **The weapons that God gives us are powerful in God for the destruction of strongholds.**

The armor we put on is not just any kind of armor. The Bible says it is the armor of God. It is not a light matter that we can handle easily. The great majority of warriors, however, have no idea how to put on this armor or how to use it.

This kind of ignorance leads people to fight the battle in the flesh. Some time ago I read an author whose name I do not remember now, saying: **"Every morning you should declare yourself dressed in the armor of God so you will be protected throughout the day."**

Unfortunately, His armor is not going to cover us just

because we make a prophetic declaration. This heavenly armor implies you are established in unconquerable heavenly positions such as truth, salvation, justice, love, faith, the preaching of the gospel, intimate communion with the revealed Word of God, in the rhemas of His Word, and from these positions you are ready to fight in the spiritual world.

This armor does not cover hypocrites who are full of falsehood and lies, and who claim to wear the belt of truth. It also does not cover unrighteous people, rebels, gossipers whose tongues are contaminated by poison, and who claim they have a heart of righteousness or a heart of love. It also does not cover those who do not have enough faith for their own finances and those who live in all sorts of fears, but nonetheless claim prophetically that they hold the shield of faith. Such people are completely ignorant and use fleshly weapons, which is ridiculous. Fighting in the flesh is like throwing axes to the moon or stones to the sun.

The armor of our God is perfect, indestructible and extremely powerful, but it only fits us to the degree we have grown into it. A warrior who fights in the Spirit of the living God is a man or a woman full of truth, who hates falsehoods and lies. He is a man full of justice and love, who continues to love in adverse and hostile circumstances.

This is a man who is full of salvation in his inner being,

who is saintly in all his ways, and who hates any kind of impurity and wickedness. He is filled with the faith of God because he knows the Lord and the Lord knows him. He has an intimate relationship with the Most High and is filled with kindness towards his brothers, full of compassion, and ready to pray under any circumstance.

This is the man or woman upon whom God will place His authority. His weapons are not man-made spears but rather swords of fire and spiritual atomic bombs in the spiritual realm. He is a soldier who acts in perfect order and within authority structure; he is trained in principles, values and submission.

A warrior clothed in meekness and humility is easy to command, both by God and be his human superiors. Such man has the fear of the Lord. He does not boast nor care about himself, because he knows the glory belongs to God alone. These are God's chosen ones; clothed in Him and armed by His Spirit. They are invincible.

6

Casualties of War

"We know that whosoever is born of God sinneth not; but he that is begotten of God keepeth himself, and that wicked one toucheth him not. And we know that we are of God, and the whole world lieth in wickedness."

-1 John 5:18, 19

1.- Who suffers accidents?

All of us in the body of Christ have experienced pain, sickness, misfortune and accidents. There are some who do not want to admit this and preach it because the devil has been defeated. He cannot do anything to us anymore, but the truth is that the church everywhere is full of sickness.

People in all Christian denominations and groups are being attacked by the devil daily. I believe it is unfair to say that sickness and adversities are results of spiritual warfare. Tragedies occur everywhere, even among those who oppose strategic warfare. Do conservative Christians never become ill or victimized by an unexpected calamity or accident?

Ever since the devil took control of the earth and established his empire of death, pain and evil, humanity has experienced great suffering. The kingdom of darkness operates by bringing suffering to both Christians and unbelievers.

> *"He that committeth sin is of the devil; for the devil sinneth from the beginning. For this purpose the Son of God was manifested, that he might destroy the works of the devil."*
>
> *-1 John 3:8*

Regardless of what satan and his demons say, there's a greater government above him which has defeated him and to whom he has to subject himself. It is certain that our enemy roams around looking for whom he may devour, but he does not have unconditional liberty to do what he wants.

Religion is an unsafe place. Indwelling in God is what keeps us from all danger.

"He who dwells in the shelter of the Most High will rest in the shadow of the Almighty. I will say of the LORD, "He is my refuge and my fortress, my God, in whom I trust." Surely he will save you from the fowler's snare and from the deadly pestilence. He will cover you with his feathers, and under his wings you will find refuge; his faithfulness will be your shield and rampart. You will not fear the terror of night, nor the arrow that flies by day, nor the pestilence that stalks in the darkness, nor the plague that destroys at midday. A thousand may fall at your side, ten thousand at your right hand, but it will not come near you. You will only observe with your eyes and see the punishment of the wicked. If you make the Most High your dwelling— even the LORD, who is my refuge, then no harm will befall you, no disaster will come near your tent. For he will command his angels concerning you to guard you in all yourways; they will lift you up in their hands, so that you will not strike your foot against a stone. You will tread upon the lion and the cobra; you will trample the great lion and the serpent. "Because he loves me," says the LORD, "I will rescue him; I will protect him, for he acknowledges my name. He will call upon

me, and I will answer him; I will be with him in trouble, I will deliver him and honor him. With long life will I satisfy him and show him my salvation."   *-Psalm 91 (NKJV)*

There are people who although they are devout Christians, but their spiritual reality is a religion believed or conceived with the mind instead of the heart. They are full of mechanisms and formulas that seem pious, but they lack the life and effectiveness of an intimate communion with God.

Being in God's Spirit is a state in which the Lord is continually transforming us, guiding and talking. It is in that spiritual state where all our trust is placed in God because we know and hear.

2 - Can the devil touch one of the anointed?

At the cross Jesus provided all the victory we will ever need to live a life that is one hundred percent protected by God.

The Word says:

"We know that whosoever is born of God sinneth not; but he that is begotten of God keepeth himself, and that wicked one toucheth him not."
                    -1 John 5:18

It also declares:

> *"Finally, my brethren, be strong in the Lord, and in the power of his might. Put on the whole armour of God, that ye may be able to stand against the wiles of the devil."*
>
> *-Ephesians 6:10, 11*

According to these sections in Scripture, it is possible to keep a permanently firm stand in the midst of evil attacks without being touched by the devil. The problem we encounter in this context is the fact that the majority of the church does not walk with the Lord as it should and therefore does not possess the entire armor of God in actual practice.

Oftentimes people believe that they do not live in sin because they are not involved in adultery or drunkenness nor do they attend pagan festivals. However, they live in religiosity, have no mercy, or are critical, and have no control over their tongues. They are full of gossip and competition and live according to their own standards instead of depending on the Holy Spirit. In many cases such people get themselves involved in spiritual warfare, and logically they are unprotected.

Any kind of sin creates an alliance with the devil and that gives the devil and his demons the legal right to touch a child of God.

a) How to discern the alliances that we might have with the enemy.

The first thing we do when we enter into spiritual warfare is to study the characteristics of the strongman we are going to fight. We list these on a blackboard and analyze them carefully. This way we gain clear understanding of the various character traits of this strongman and begin to see which of these traits are present in our own lives; ways in which we have come to identify with the character of this spirit.

I believe one of Paul's errors which almost brought him total defeat when he preached the gospel in Athens, was the strategy he used when he entered the capital.

The strongman or the ruling spirit was the spirit of Greece. Its characteristics among many other things are: intellectualism, humanism, a cult which puts reason above the spirit, eloquence, arrogance, the habit to always demonstrate that you know more than others, and never ending discussions which focus on proving everything logically.

Without realizing it, Paul fell into a trap of this spirit and became involved in it. His preaching was intellectual without any manifestation of power and the results were almost zero.

"Now while Paul waited for them at Athens, his spirit was stirred in him, when he saw the city wholly given to idolatry. Therefore disputed he in the synagogue with the Jews, and with the devout persons, and in the market daily with them that met with him. Then certain philosophers of the Epicureans, and of the Stoicks, encountered him. And some said, What will this babbler say? other some, He seemeth to be a setter forth of strange gods: because he preached unto them Jesus, and the resurrection."   *- Acts 17:16-18*

Notice how Paul already begins to bow to this spirit of discussion, and then he walks into the trap of the enemy, by falling into an intellectual argument:

"And they took him, and brought him unto Areopagus, saying, May we know what this new doctrine, whereof thou speakest, is? For thou bringest certain strange things to our ears: we would know therefore what these things mean. (For all the Athenians and strangers which were there spent their time in nothing else, but either to tell, or to hear some new thing.)"

    – Acts 17:19-21

The Greeks did not seek God, nor were their hearts simple enough to receive salvation. Their minds were held captive by this territorial spirit, and they were able to ensnare Paul in their game.

The Apostle, after an eloquent discourse about the "Unknown God," receives scorn and ridicule from the Athenians and ends up with only a small group of believers in that city.

Paul's reaction to this defeat, of which he was clearly aware of, was to enter Corinth in a totally opposite spirit. It is obvious to me from the manner in which he spoke to the Corinthians that he must have had a strong encounter with the Holy Spirit between his visit to Athens and his visit to Corinth.

Take note of the radical change in his preaching:

"And I, brethren, when I came to you, came not with excellency of speech or of wisdom, declaring unto you the testimony of God. For I determined not to know any thing among you, save Jesus Christ, and him crucified. And I was with you in weakness, and in fear, and in much trembling. And my speech and my preaching was not with enticing words of man's wisdom, but in demonstration of the Spirit and of power."

1 Corinthians 2:1-4

What he did was to act in a spirit that is opposite to the

spirit of Greece; hereby cutting every alliance with the mindset and personality that is associated with that spirit. Contrary to the wisdom of the Greeks, he decided to know nothing except Jesus Christ. Instead of arrogance, he presented himself with fear and trembling. Instead of discussions, he demonstrated the simplicity and the power of God. This resulted in a church that attracted many people, and he was able to raise strong disciples in this area.

In our own situation, when we fight against territorial forces it is very important to study how they act. Then we have to break all alliances in our souls that tie up with the characteristics of those forces and then operate in exactly the opposite spirit.

For example, if we are going to fight against the "queen of the heaven" or the great Babylon, the first thing Scripture says about this is:

> *"Then I heard another voice calling from heaven,*
> *"Come away from her, my people. Do not take*
> *part in her sins, or you will be punished with*
> *her."*   *- Revelation 18:4 (NKJV)*

What we do next is we infer from the Bible and from history all the possible character traits of each queen Scripture speaks about. Without making an exhaustive list, here are some of them:

Queen Vashti. She was vain and did not respect authority. She put her ego above the will of her husband. She found it easy to disobey and she was rebellious. Her concerns were more important than those of anyone else, to mention a few or her character traits.

Queen Jezebel. She was manipulative and ruled over her husband. She was opposed to the prophetic voice, had no fear of God, was idolatrous and considered herself a prophetess. She seduced the servants of God into fornication and the consumption of things sacrificed to idols.

She made them feel that fornication and compromising the Word of God was acceptable. She made them enjoy sin. She made them feel good in the midst of their sins. She was a trickster and always had to have things go her way. She had to impose her will at any price even if it meant the destruction of someone else. She was a terrible idolatress and associated with the python, which is a spirit in the form of an asp. This spirit annihilates with its tongue by releasing deadly venom. It strangles and suffocates its victims until they do what it demands from them.

The Queen of Sheba. She buys grace with presents. She's a seductress, very sensual, a flatterer, who seeks positions of greatness by giving favors, services and gifts.

Queen Athaliah sought position, power and seniority,

and destroys whomever she needs to destroy (both in the spiritual and the natural). She lords it over everyone and there was no one who opposes her.

There are others, but I do not pretend to make a profound study of the queen of heaven but to establish a principle which serves to make us untouchable in the battle.

The vast majority of warriors and intercessors are extremely dedicated to God. They make much effort in prayer, spend nights without sleep, seek revelation and are faithful witnesses. They love God very much and will do anything for Him. All this however, does not free them from danger. If the apostle Paul could be ensnared by a spirit which brought failure to him, the same thing can happen to us.

In my experience with thousands of intercessors and soldiers of the Most High God, I've seen that they believe it is enough to focus on the qualities and spiritual gifts God gave them, and to do humbly whatever God asks them to do.

When the devil sees people with wonderful characters, he will look for subtle openings in them that can give him legal ground to attack them. For this reason God showed us how important it is to analyze and scrutinize ourselves so that we can identify those characteristics in us that we share with the territorial spirits. It's easy to say, "I'm a devoted servant of God. I don't have anything in common with Jezebel." However, God demands us to look deeply into our human nature. If we are sincere enough to admit it, all of us have characteristics like control, manipulation, rebellion and vanity, among many other things. The simple reason for this is that we come from a fallen race which has shaped our character and soul.

From the time a baby is born, he or she starts to manipulate. The first word most children learn, after the words mammy and daddy, is "no!" The baby is not even aware of its own name, yet he knows how to impose its own will. Little by little the child will discover what his parents' tolerance levels are and how to manipulate them in order to get his or her way.

If anyone wants to know how Jezebel operates in your life, then observe how you react to radical opposition to the most important goal in your life. Some react with anger and vengeance, others with sadness and depression and yet others with cunning. The objective of all of these various reactions is manipulation and control. It is necessary to recognize this and ask for forgiveness so the devil cannot touch us.

This is in fact the primary manifestation of the queen of heaven in us. Such is man's nature: rebellious, disobedient, controlling and full of evil. The great majority of intercessors and warriors are guided by the Holy Spirit and sanctified in many ways. But, believe me, we have not even begun to scratch the surface of the soul. There may be issues that we sincerely believe have been pardoned and no longer work in us, whereas they have never really been confessed nor have been remitted by anyone.

When our battle team looks for alliances with the character traits of the spirit we are about to fight, we take considerable time to discuss with one another and to bring to light any previous action that is related to these character traits. We review even our most distant past; the thoughts that crossed our minds, the movies or television programs we watched in which we admired a hero with such character traits. Sometimes God will remind us of jokes we have told or listened to and laughed at in the past, which created an alliance with that particular spirit. I'm not suggesting you should turn off your television for the rest of your life or never tell a joke. I'm saying that we must seek to recognize the weakness of our human nature, which is still on the road to perfection.

I remember a dear warrior who stood up during our preparation for war at the concentration camp in Auschwitz, while we were analyzing the characteristics of the spirit of Hitler. She said: "I definitely do not identify with the anti-Semitic spirit of Hitler." Then there was silence, which was broken by another companion who said to her: "Remember how we used to laugh in school at those jokes about

Auschwitz." She repented, and we all saw clearly how easily we may develop subtle points of identification with the work of the devil.

Furthermore, the extent to which we recognize these alliances, which seemed so insignificant before, is the extent to which we gain a position of spiritual authority from where we can fight without danger. Ever since we understood this principle and carried it out, we have not had a single casualty of war. Perhaps this is not highly relevant for a common churchgoing Christian, but it is of course very relevant for a warrior who fights against territorial powers.

b) The devil can touch us when we lack proper order.

Territorial warfare is a delicate matter. We can compare this war to a campaign in which the best intelligence services in the entire world work together. In a military conflict in the natural world, the victory or defeat of each opponent depends on who has:

-The best strategy
-The greatest knowledge of the strengths and weaknesses of the opponent.
-The best organized army
-The most powerful weapons
This order is certainly very important. As the children of God we possess the most powerful weapons. Nevertheless,

many battles have been lost due to poor strategy and lack of knowledge as to where the attack of the enemy is coming from.

Let us compare this to a chess game where you have to anticipate the deceptive moves of your enemy, and to stay alert and vigilant so you can prevent these moves before he actually makes them.

Warfare requires divine intelligence, shrewdness, intuition and revelation. You need to know precisely when and where you are going to attack. Do not drop bombs like a madman just when you encounter a stronghold, because the ways to fight and destroy targets are not always the same. Making this kind of mistake can carry a very high price.

It is important in all warfare that we can count on organized armies. Their generals and captains have to be in harmony and agreement. Every part of the army needs to be prepared and sanctified, and needs to be sufficiently covered by fasting and prayer before and after the battle. Spiritual mapping and prophetic words must throw light on the correct battle strategy. The participants must be people who accept authority and are totally submitted.

Warriors who act on their own initiative and who long to be heroes will endanger the entire army. If people within the army are involved in sin, this will create openings for the entire army to be defeated. This happened in the battle against Ai, Joshua's army lost this battle due to Achan's transgression (reference Joshua 8).

There is a basic principle of warfare. According to this principle the level in which we can attack the devil is directly related to the level of our authority and the level of our relationship with the Lord. The deeper our relationship with God is, the higher the level will be in which we can do warfare against principalities.

A warrior who wants to fight against territorial forces but lacks the power to deliver someone possessed by demons, logically does not have the power necessary to fight at a high level.

The person who desires to do high level warfare but is unable to overcome his character flaws or his own financial situation, does not have such power either, but will be easily defeated.

In order to confront powers at high levels you need an authority that has been tested by fire and you must have an extremely strong relationship with God.

The combined strength of many mighty warriors serves as a fortress protecting the weaker member of the group. Do not try to eliminate a warrior because of some slight weakness but rather try to help, protect and support him to grow through the shared experience of the rest of the group.

We do not acquire ranks in the army of God on the basis of how much revelation we receive but on the basis of the victories we have won over the enemy. The fall of a powerful principality catapults the warrior into a greater sphere of influence in the spiritual world.

Our authority as part of the army of God is also intimately related to the degree to which we submit to our earthly authorities. At times people are called to spiritual warfare but are members of a church where the subject is not familiar or is even rejected. In the first case, the warrior has to inform his pastor of his calling to be a part of the spiritual army of God. If his pastor is open he will explore the issue and allow the soldier to be prepared by others who have more experience and who have a proven ministry in this area.

In the second case, the soldier will have to decide whether he should forget the war and remain serving his pastor or whether he should leave that church and look for a place where he can grow as a spiritual warrior.

To sense the calling without respecting the authority of the pastors is extremely dangerous and has actually resulted in the destruction of many warriors. They go into combat as martyrs for God. They go into battle without understanding the government that the Lord has put in place over the church. This is wrong and certainly not the will of God.

Our God is a God of order and He submits to His own designs. The Lord raises someone up for territorial warfare because he has had previous training. God connects this person to generals and places him in their care so they can help him. Though there will be opposition, most of the doors of opportunity will open and God's plans will prosper in accordance with His will.

In my organization there are warriors who are members of other churches where spiritual warfare is not practiced. However, their pastors agree that I cover them in matters of warfare so they can grow according to their calling. To have this covering the soldier must be in perfect subjection to his pastoral or apostolic authority. When he engages in combat, he submits his strategies to me and we cover him with our intercessory network.

The level of covering must correspond with the level of warfare we engage in; this is very important. For example, we cannot fight against a national principality under the covering of one small independent church. On the other hand, we cannot fight against a worldwide power of darkness when our intercessory covering is at a national level. It is necessary and indispensable that this type of war effort is covered by a worldwide ministry.

I'm personally submitted to apostle Rony Chaves of Costa Rica. But in matters of warfare in the United States and Europe the apostle C. Peter Wagner functions as my covering. In general I am accountable to both persons for my life and actions.

Since my conversion, I've been called to spiritual warfare, which required a very tough training and treatment from God. This raised me up to fight battles against high level principalities and powers. I can see that from the beginning God designed everything for my growth. I was born in a church that was very strong in deliverance during that time and was extremely radical in its dealings with sin and the flesh. Since my very first steps as a Christian, this church taught me to live a life nailed to the cross, but it also trained me in the power of God and in the area of faith.

God Himself was the one who placed me besides His servants who were indispensable in my development. I had great teachers, beginning with my father in the ministry, Dr. Morris Cerullo, who believed in me and who trained me extensively under his ministry. Besides him, God provided others who each became a necessary part in my formation.

I can tell you with all certainty that any high level warrior is forged as a sword of steel in the same way, in ovens with intense fire; where he receives blow upon blow by the hammer until his blades are sharp and shining. There is no such thing as a microwave warrior who, after one powerful seminar, is ready to go out and perform mighty deeds.

3. Accidents of war or suffering from God?

An accident of war is considered as a casualty, a fatality, an unfortunate event or as an attack of the devil. As we have previously seen, it is possible to have assurance of God's protection so that the attacks of the devil will not prosper in our lives.

I believe our focus should not be on what satan might do as a result of war. But, we must look at situations from a correct viewpoint, because we cannot claim that everything that happens to us is "a counterattack from the enemy".

The Apostle John wrote:

"We know that whoever is born of God sins not; but he that is begotten of God keeps himself, and that wicked one touches him not."
- 1 John 5:18 (NKJV)

According to history this same apostle John was submerged in boiling oil and was jailed in the island of Patmos and suffered in many other ways. Nevertheless, he never entertained the thought that the devil could touch him.

Jesus said:

"Behold, I give unto you power to tread on serpents and scorpions, and over all the power of the enemy: and nothing shall by any means hurt you.."   *- Luke 10:19*

He knew that the church would be tortured, persecuted, and suffer martyrdom and yet, He did not attribute these works to the devil.

When Paul suffered various tribulations, God revealed to him that he should not look at things in the natural but to focus on what is happening in the invisible world. From this perspective each present affliction contributes to the weight of the eternal glory that was growing in his inner man. (Paraphrase from 2 Corinthians 4:16-18).

What happened during the greatest battle ever fought, which ended on the cross of Calvary? In the natural eyes of man, when Jesus died, satan had won the war. This is to say, he managed to have Jesus tortured, humiliated, severely abused and in the end, killed.

If we consider this only from a natural viewpoint, and from the external appearance of things, it looks like this is a terrible attack by the evil one in which he defeated Jesus and nothing more than that. But what happened in the invisible world, which could only have been perceived by the mind of God was that through His death, He conquered death and sin. Through His pain, He conquered pain; through experiencing violent abuse, He conquered violent abuse; through His humility, He conquered arrogance and through all this terrible suffering, He annihilated the empire of the devil.

What looked like utter defeat (because at that moment no one believed Jesus would be resurrected) and put an end to all of their hopes was in reality the biggest victory in the entire universe. What appeared as a surprise attack from satan against the Son of God was in fact a design from the Father, which was planned before the creation of the world.

To see only the external part of things, to see analytically and logically with our minds, will inevitably lead to spiritual errors.

It is quite possible that God is creating the most marvelous work in our lives in the midst of what we might consider a great tragedy. We do not realize this because we always put the blame on the devil and focus only on the negative side of things. This is exactly what the evil one wants us to do, so that he can keep the people of God under a yoke of fear. This problem started when God's point of view and that of the church became totally opposed to each other during the twentieth and twenty-first centuries. The modern world which includes most churches, lives under a system which is oriented to comfort, well-being and the immediate satisfaction of the soul. The people in the world are bombarded every day by thousands of advertisements with subliminal messages binding them to a consumerism that is out of control. Whether we like it or not, this entire system affects the common denominator of what the present day church thinks. Our entire environment originates from this system and screams: "Avoid suffering at all cost!" The world will do anything to avoid suffering or to suffer as little as possible.

However, the way God thinks about our tribulations is very different. God knows that our main enemy is not the devil, because God already defeated him. Our main enemies are our own flesh, our own ego, and our friendship with the world, which turn us into enemies of God. He knows that the best thing for us is to die to all of these as soon as possible.

From divine perspective the most valuable thing that can happen to us is to die to everything that separates us from God or from His destiny for us. For God, suffering is just a mild, momentary tribulation through which He will make us grow in maturity, as He reveals increasing levels of glory of His kingdom and allows us to enter them. "It is necessary that you enter the kingdom of God after many tribulations."

The devil does not have any authority to do as he

pleases against any child of God, nor in the midst of any war. He is subject to and at the service of the Most High God. Jesus reminded him of this in the desert:

> *"And Jesus answered and said unto him, Get thee behind me, Satan: for it is written, Thou shalt worship the Lord thy God, and him only shalt thou serve."*   *- Luke 4:8*

Job suffered tremendous tribulation due to satan's attacks. However, all this terrible suffering was not originated by satan nor was it an accident of spiritual warfare, but came from God:

> *"And the LORD said unto Satan, Whence comest thou? Then Satan answered the LORD, and said, From going to and fro in the earth, and from walking up and down in it. And the LORD said unto Satan, Hast thou considered my servant Job, that there is none like him in the earth, a perfect and an upright man, one that feareth God, and escheweth evil? Then Satan answered the LORD, and said, Doth Job fear God for nought? Hast not thou made an hedge about him, and about his house, and about all that he hath on every side? thou hast blessed the work of his hands, and his substance is increased in the land. But put forth thine hand now, and touch all that he hath, and he will curse thee to thy face. And*

the LORD said unto Satan, Behold, all that he
hath is in thy power; only upon himself put not
forth thine hand. So Satan went forth from the
presence of the LORD."

- Job 1:7-12

The book of Job tells us how he lost everything, (family, blessings, health) and also how God worked powerfully in his life. The Lord had a glorious design for Job, but He knew Job could obtain the level of knowing Him that God had prepared for him only through deep tribulation.

God was always in control of everything. Satan was never going to be on the winning side in this battle, not even in Job's worse suffering. God was always the one who lifted the banner of triumph in the spiritual realm until this triumph was expressed through the total transformation of Job and his prosperity. God always had Job's welfare in mind. His eyes were focused on the marvelous purpose He was working out in the life of His servant.

We see a similar case when satan asked Jesus if he could sift Peter like wheat. Of course satan cannot give orders to Jesus. Jesus already had a glorious plan for His disciple, but it would be fulfilled only through tremendous shaking of the soul. Jesus approved the devil's action whereas He was going to pray that Peter's faith would not fail.

For some time Peter walked through hell; he was absolutely desperate because he denied Jesus. As a result of his tribulation, his inner man was purified so that he could later strengthen the brethren.

It is written:
"If we suffer, we shall also reign with him: if we deny him, he also will deny us."
- 2 Timothy 2:12

It is also written:
"The Spirit itself beareth witness with our spirit, that we are the children of God: And if children, then heirs; heirs of God, and joint-heirs with Christ; if so, be that we suffer with him, that we may be also glorified together."
- Romans 8:16, 17

Suffering was the way of life for the early church; it was adopted by the apostles so that the message of the cross would reach the farthest ends of the earth. They did not seek to avoid pain but rather understood the deep level of glory suffering would bring.

Notice how different the understanding of the apostle Paul was compared to that of our end time's Christian churches.

"Yea doubtless, and I count all things but loss for

the excellency of the knowledge of Christ Jesus my Lord: for whom I have suffered the loss of all things, and do count them but dung, that I may win Christ, And be found in him, not having mine own righteousness, which is of the law, but that which is through the faith of Christ, the righteousness which is of God by faith: That I may know him, and the power of his resurrection, and the fellowship of his sufferings, being made conformable unto his death."

- Philippians 3:8-10

Paul also said:

"But we have this treasure in earthen vessels, that the excellency of the power may be of God, and not of us. We are troubled on every side, yet not distressed; we are perplexed, but not in despair; Persecuted, but not forsaken; cast down, but not destroyed; Always bearing about in the body the dying of the Lord Jesus, that the life also of Jesus might be made manifest in our body. For we which live are always delivered unto death for Jesus' sake, that the life also of Jesus might be made manifest in our mortal flesh."

- 2 Corinthians 4:7-11

What superior understanding, what a sublime focus! Here we see someone who knows what he is looking for;

whose goals are heavenly. His objective is to let the resurrection life and power of Jesus become manifest and shine in his fleshly body, so that all the world literally could see Jesus in him.

He was not preoccupied with the devil stealing his car or breaking his bones. His values did not concern the loss of freedom or his life. He got to this point because God told him:

"And he said unto me, My grace is sufficient for thee: for my strength is made perfect in weakness. Most gladly therefore will I rather glory in my infirmities, that the power of Christ may rest upon me. Therefore I take pleasure in infirmities, in reproaches, in necessities, in persecutions, in distresses for Christ's sake: for when I am weak, then am I strong." - *2 Corinthians 12:9, 10*

For him, everything was gain. Death was the victory he longed for and which would put him on the same level of power as his beloved Jesus. He was inclined to suffer everything in order to evangelize the lost. He was a true soldier of the Lord, a general whose example inspires us and fills us with the boldness and compassion to fight for the nations.

Paul knew, like the other disciples, that the advancement

of God's kingdom carried a very high price. The simple act of snatching a soul from the devil could, and still can, transform a society or even an entire region in the kingdom of darkness!

When John and Peter healed the lame man at the temple gates (which were called Beautiful), it resulted in an uproar in Jerusalem so that both of them were detained. Paul's preaching in the city of Ephesus created a riot in the entire city, which turned against him. Stephen preached only one time and it cost him his life.

It is not only spiritual warfare at a territorial level that disturbs the devil's kingdom, but also the advancement of the true light into the darkness. There are divine designs that have to do with suffering inflicted on us, such as the loss of a loved one, loss of health or the loss of all our possession. Never, at any time, do these losses mean that the devil has won in a counterattack.

Take for example the amazing way Jesus established His church during the first century. The gospel spread but His followers were martyred, thrown before the lions, crucified, burned and tortured. The thoughts of those martyred were not centered on "Let's stop attending these meetings because the devil will attack and martyr us." On the contrary, the more the believers were subject to execution the more the church grew and the more powerful it became.

According to God's designs, which are infinitely wiser than ours, the shedding of blood that occurred at that time was necessary. The power of the blood of those martyrs laid such a strong foundation that the church was able to survive up to this time.

Through the sacrifice of each martyr, the power of the Roman Empire became increasingly weakened until it completely collapsed. This was certainly spiritual warfare at a very high level. In the mind of natural man the loss of life is a great tragedy, but for God it is the highest form of promotion.

I have been doing spiritual warfare since 1989 and have suffered all kinds of losses: close and dear beloved ones whom the Lord called to His presence. Among them was my closest family: my twin sister. I know without a doubt that none of this happened due to counterattacks from a troublesome devil since God is able to control him. But they happened because of His glorious designs for my life. I remember when my sister Mercedes departed to glory. God very clearly spoke to me: "I'm forming a powerful army who will serve alongside my angels, and it's necessary that one of you fight from the heavens and the other one from the earth." She was the fortunate one! And when my turn comes to leave this world I'll know all the wonderful things that the Lord assigned her to do.

In Jesus, heaven and earth are the same and Mercedes

is filled with glory as she is waiting for me holding her arms wide. Most certainly she intercedes for me through all my battles. I haven't lost anything, nor has the devil stolen her away from me. Mercedes has simply changed her address and, in a few years time, I will see her again.

I say again that the problem is rooted in our tendency to look at issues of divine order from a human perspective. We live in an electronic age where almost everything is solved with the push of a button. This is very true in countries that are highly developed. We also try to implement similar solutions when we try to establish the kingdom of God here on earth. We want a technological gospel where the earth will be filled with the glory of God just by turning a key or pressing a button. We want a gospel of blessings and prosperity, and we propagate everything that has to do with worldly success and what sounds good to the ear. The most important thing to us is peace, security and wealth in this world. This is unfortunately, the description of the church in Laodicea revealed to John in the Book of Revelation, when he refers to the church of Laodicea. He showed him that this church felt wealthy and not needing anything. Yet in God's eyes its true condition was characterized by poverty, misery, blindness, wretchedness and nakedness.

It is a terrible thing for a church if it fits this description. This church becomes an easy target for a lying and intimidating devil that wants to fill it with fear, and many times succeeds in doing so. This church becomes easily frightened and egoistic, and therefore loses its sensitivity and genuine compassion.

Please forgive me for writing like this but God wants to lift His church into higher dimensions. God wants to lift our understanding and power, and in order to accomplish this, it is necessary to face reality and make radical changes.

7

Attacks from the devil or correction from God?

"Submit yourselves therefore to God. Resist the devil, and he will flee from you. Draw nigh to God, and he will draw nigh to you. Cleanse your hands, ye sinners; and purify your hearts, ye double minded."   *-James 4:7, 8*

1.- Warfare exposes us to the glory and the justice of God.

W e cannot begin to discuss high level warfare without acknowledging that every battle begins at the throne of God. It is God who determines how long each military conflict in the heavenly places will last. It is not up to us to determine the times or seasons, but it is up to God alone. The times are intimately connected with the establishment of God's justice and His judgments.

Every war is a judgment that God uses to bring:

a) Freedom to the oppressed.
b) Punishment or destruction to the oppressors.
c) To establish God's justice.

In order to carry out a judgment a legal framework is required. God's main objective is to establish His justice in a territory so that all the goodness of His kingdom can be manifested.

> *"The LORD reigneth; let the earth rejoice; let the multitude of isles be glad thereof. Clouds and darkness are round about him: righteousness and judgment are the habitation of his throne. A fire goeth before him, and burneth up his enemies round about. The heavens declare his righteousness, and all the people see his glory."*
>
> *- Psalms 97:1-3 and 6*

We find in this psalm a fundamental principle that makes us understand that God takes the initiative in the warfare against His enemies. Our role in starting a battle is to make room for the manifestation of God's throne in a place. For this purpose the saints need to pray, fast and cry out to God. When God hears an effective and genuine outcry, He will reveal His throne to the prophets which will be the signal that we can approach the throne and ask Him to judge our enemies.

In the case of Israel's deliverance from the hands of the Egyptian Pharaoh, God waited until the abominations of the Amorites had reached their peak. This was the time that He had determined to carry out justice. He heard the outcry of four hundred years of oppression and then, He revealed Himself to Moses in the burning bush.

> *"And he said unto Abram, Know of a surety that thy seed shall be a stranger in a land that is not theirs, and shall serve them; and they shall afflict them four hundred years; And also that nation, whom they shall serve, will I judge: and afterward shall they come out with great substance. But in the fourth generation they shall come hither again: for the iniquity of the Amorites is not yet full."*
> — Genesis 15:13, 14 and 16

It is extremely important to understand that, before we engage in battle, we need an encounter with the glory of God, with His throne, or with a manifestation of the angel of the Lord. I have learned that it is necessary to enter warfare in fear and trembling before God.

Many times when we sense an extreme need or when we discern a horrible demonic power in a place, it gives us a strong desire to go into combat. But it is necessary that we wait for Him. When His glory is revealed, we know it is safe to go to battle.

God wants to give us the nations today. This is the time of the great harvest and of the deliverance of the peoples of the earth. Even so, He is still the King and the Supreme Commander of His troops.

Joshua had a marvelous encounter with the prince of the armies of Jehovah when he was going to take the Promised Land.

> "And it came to pass, when Joshua was by Jericho, that he lifted up his eyes and looked, and, behold, there stood a man over against him with his sword drawn in his hand: and Joshua went unto him, and said unto him, Art thou for us, or for our adversaries? And he said, Nay; but as captain of the host of the LORD am I now come. And Joshua fell on his face to the earth, and did worship, and said unto him, What saith my lord unto his servant? And the captain of the LORD'S host said unto Joshua, Loose thy shoe from off thy foot; for the place whereon thou standest is holy. And Joshua did so."
>
> - Joshua 5:13-15

Not only the appearance of this prince is relevant, who is none other than Jesus Christ in His pre-incarnate form, but also the very certain "no" of his answer.

Regarding this response, the prophet Rick Joyner writes

in his book The Final Quest, what Jesus told him: "When I judge, I'm not looking to condemn or justify, what I bring is My justice. My justice is found only among those who are in unity with Me. This is a right justice: to bring mankind into union with Me.

"When I appeared before Joshua as the Prince of the armies of God, I told him I wasn't on his side or on the side of his enemies. I don't take sides. When I return, it's to take into account all circumstances, not to take the side of anyone. I appeared as the Prince of the armies of God when Israel was going to enter the Promised Land. The Church is about to enter its Promised Land and again, I reveal Myself as the Prince of the armies. When I do this, I will take out of the way all those who have forced my people to take part in any issue that has pitted one against the other. My justice doesn't take sides in human conflicts, especially not in those that exist among my people. What I did for Israel, I was also doing for her enemies, not against them. You look at things from a temporal, terrestrial viewpoint and it doesn't allow you to see My justice. It's necessary for you to see My justice so that you can walk in My authority, because justice and judgment are the foundation of my throne."

For this reason it was vitally important that all the people who participated in the battle were circumcised and sanctified.

Note, how God spoke the same words both to Moses and to Joshua before a great judgment came upon their enemies: "Take off your sandals, for this is holy ground." It is as if God Himself absorbed His chosen ones into His glorious Holiness, in order to enable them to bring destruction to His enemies.

This is exactly the manifestation of His throne, of the seat of His government from where He issues the execution of His judgments. Later on, we will see how the glory of God and His justice are intimately involved in the destruction of the oppressor. We can see this same principle operating in the judgment of the great Babylon in the book of Revelation:

> *"And after these things I saw another angel come down from heaven, having great power; and the earth was lightened with his glory. And he cried mightily with a strong voice, saying, Babylon the great is fallen, is fallen, and is become the habitation of devils, and the hold of every foul spirit, and a cage of every unclean and hateful bird. Therefore shall her plagues come in one day, death, and mourning, and famine; and she shall be utterly burned with fire: for strong is the Lord God who judgeth her."*
>
> *- Revelation 18:1, 2, and 8*

Here we see the angel of glory announcing the powerful judgment of the great harlot.

The principle that we should understand is that we cannot ask for vengeance against our enemies without understanding how the glory, justice and judgment operate. God will not smash our enemies without first exposing us to His justice and the glory. In a war it is the manifestation of the glory of God that destroys the power of the devil.

The glory is so impressively holy that it will burn everything that is impure and break it into pieces. Do not think the devil can easily come near the radiant glory of God. This is why the Lord is preparing an army that is truly immersed in the magnificent splendor of His presence.

When God raised us up for warfare on a strategic territorial level, there was hardly anyone who followed us. We were pioneers in the things that: "No eye has seen, nor ear has heard, and no mind has imagined what God has prepared for those who love Him."

In the beginning, this calling required tremendous steps of obedience and at times these steps felt like jumps into empty space, hoping that God would be there with His arms open so that we would not fall. I realize now that we committed many errors, but in His grace and mercy He sustained us, while He taught us to become spearheads of the powerful army that He was raising up. The further we advanced in His divine training, the more we experienced His requirements upon us. He began to demand more and tolerate less. Little by little He began to correct the mistakes we committed in the beginning and subject them to discipline, so that at the end of our training we could train others.

I became aware of something that systematically happened after each war. During combat we were clothed in a very powerful light; this was the power of God which allowed us to win. However, after the battle, the same light turned on us and exposed and revealed whatever wrong attitudes or sins the warriors still had. Nothing remained hidden. After our return from war we lived under God's light. It became very evident to us that we entered a level of sanctification that belonged to His military order.

I also began to realize that the more difficult the operation is, and the higher the level of territorial forces we fight, the higher the level of God's manifested glory becomes.

It became clear to me that the glory did not only attack the enemies of God, but we were subjected to the same level of glory with which God fought in our favor. The light exposes but the glory burns.

God sanctified us in way that was both marvelous

and very painful. An encounter with God's spot light (as I call it) showed our shortcomings; those attitudes that are so difficult to see. This enables us to confess and repent for our sins. His glory was an intense fiery experience. On the one hand God judged our enemies, but on the other hand He subjected us to the intensive tests of His purifying fire. The price for warfare became extremely high, but we also experienced His glory and marvelous majesty.

Many times we have seen God face to face. We have been taken into the heavens on numerous occasions. The glory makes us one with Him. The conversations I now have with my beloved Master and King are delightful and plenteous. I would not exchange these heavenly treasures for anything.

He has filled me with the wisdom and understanding to know that when God fights a war, the devil cannot counterattack. When the magnificent glory of the Most High is released over the territories of evil, believe me, satan will not dare to face such a devastating presence.

As Scripture says:

> *"Submit yourselves therefore to God. Resist the devil, and he will flee from you. Draw nigh to God, and he will draw nigh to you. Cleanse your hands, ye sinners; and purify your hearts, ye double minded."* — *James 4:7, 8*

If he flees only because you resist him, what do you think he will do when he is judged by the glory of God? I tell you the truth, the last thing he wants to do is to counterattack.

When you do warfare in the flesh, be careful! Surely you will experience retaliation. The issue is not what the devil will do after the battle, but what God is going to do. There may be crooked ways in our lives that we cannot see, and sometimes we have to suffer the loss of possessions and loved ones so that the full blessing of His justice becomes manifest in our lives.

I remember that after having fought a war, my best friend died at that time. It hurt very much but for several months the Lord showed me little by little how this friendship had affected, in the wrong way, my destiny with Him. He is now with the Lord and I am much better now than I was then. Some would say: "This was a casualty of war; an attack from the evil one." But the truth is that it was God's liberating work and His way of perfecting my life.

As human beings, we are tied to the comforts of this life and the tangible things of this world. There are many people who literally, idolize their possessions or their families. Their children or their spouses become the foundation of their happiness and they give them a higher place in their lives than God. God has to shake these foundations in order fulfill their destinies and to lift them to higher levels of His glory. Such work is not from the devil. It is God's work because of His great love for us.

On one occasion, as I returned from a big battle, one of my main warriors was diagnosed with cancer of the uterus. She had been married to a man who had betrayed her and wounded her heart terribly. Although she had pardoned him on a conscious level, the sickness made her search her heart deeply once again in order to beat the cancer. During the healing process God took her to unimaginably deep levels of her soul. She managed to forgive from the very root, which healed all the inner pain that was caused by her husband; it was deeply rooted in her sexual life, and affected her uterus. She not only conquered the sickness, but also passed this test with a mighty heart that can face great battles.

Today she has a powerful ministry which helps hundreds of people who are bound by drugs, witchcraft and vandalism. She is a woman of great courage; she was exposed to the glory and came out shining.

Thanks to such purification which is both horrible and marvelous, we acquire the rank to fight in the heavenly places. Authority is not just a theological position of victory in Christ, but it is also forged and obtained through fire. No moment will be more glorious than when God takes you by the hand and says:

*"To him that overcometh will I grant to sit with
me in my throne, even as I also overcame, and
am set down with my Father in his throne."*

- Revelation 3:21

God grants this prize to those who win, to those who
emerge from the lukewarm state and conformity that
characterized the church in Laodicea.

The church is crying out for a manifestation of God and
for His justice and the destruction of its enemies. Certainly
He will come and establish His justice in the nations. But
before this happens, we first have to submit to the flame
of His glory.

*"Behold, I will send my messenger, and he shall
prepare the way before me: and the Lord, whom
ye seek, shall suddenly come to his temple, even
the messenger of the covenant, whom ye delight
in: behold, he shall come, saith the LORD of
hosts. But who may abide the day of his coming?
and who shall stand when he appeareth? for he
is like a refiner's fire, and like fullers' soap: And
he shall sit as a refiner and purifier of silver: and
he shall purify the sons of Levi, and purge them
as gold and silver, that they may offer unto the
LORD an offering in righteousness. Then shall
the offering of Judah and Jerusalem be pleasant
unto the LORD, as in the days of old, and as in*

former years. And I will come near to you to judgment; and I will be a swift witness against the sorcerers, and against the adulterers, and against false swearers, and against those that oppress the hireling in his wages, the widow, and the fatherless, and that turn aside the stranger from his right, and fear not me, saith the LORD of hosts."
- Malachi 3:1-5

2. Can the devil really counterattack in fight that God has already won?

In the previous paragraphs I established the premise that the devil cannot counterattack in a battle that God has already won. Wherever I go people always ask me: "If we go to war, how do we protect ourselves against counterattacks?"

When we profoundly study this subject in the Bible, which is the anchor of our foundations, we see that there is not a single battle in which God gained victory over His enemies and then the adversary rises up and counterattack.

Victory was always achieved when:

-God spoke to His prophets that He was going to give His enemies into the hands of His army.

-When the people lived in holiness and obedience to God.

Every time God won the war, the enemy was crushed and defeated. It was not like the horror movies that are shown today, in which the murderer is killed innumerable times but always comes back to life as if nothing has happened.

This is unfortunately the way things go according to the lies of Hollywood. In the spiritual world however, things go differently. When God wins the battle, the victory is complete.

It is the same in the natural world. When a war is won, the army that has lost is captured or completely destroyed; just analyze history. This does not mean that in the future no new wars will break out. But these military conflicts will be different ones; with different conditions and with other people involved.

In the Bible the army of Israel lost its wars due to the following causes:

a) The people fought in their own strength. In other words, they did not consult Jehovah.

b) God announced its defeat beforehand; it was a judgment of Israel.

c)There was disobedience in the middle of the war, for which reason God left the army of Israel.

d) In one particular case, the enemy sacrificed its first born son and Israel simply withdrew from the battle without suffering any loss in its army. (- 2 Kings 3)

3. Attacks during the conflict

I definitely believe the devil cannot counterattack while we are immersed in God's glory and obtain the victory. However, things are different during the battle or when we are still preparing.

In my experience with innumerable battles I have seen the devil attack before the war begins. He will do anything to persuade us that we should not confront him in battle. At that moment the glory has not yet manifested; everything is still in a preparatory stage and that is when he begins to shoot his arrows.

From the human perspective the skirmishes before the war are in fact the most difficult part. Once God and His angels enter the combat, warfare becomes a marvelous experience. Of course it is exhausting at times and it requires impressive tenacity and courage, but it is always glorious.

It is possible to be under intense attack from the moment the battle begins up to its very end. But I believe that we will not be touched if we continue to be immersed in Jesus and in the splendor of His glory. In some wars His glory manifests so powerfully that the enemies turn against each other and we do nothing else but glorify God.

The first battle we have to win is the battle of faith and resistance. In this stage God truly prepares His army. God will deal with us in a very direct manner. He refines us and places us in positions of authority in order to be able to win the war. This requires that we have the complete armor and power of God.

It is as if God places us in a camp for high level military training and those who do not pass the training would not be ready to go to battle.

When we trained for our climb to Mount Everest, we did not merely focus on the practice of climbing and a good physical condition but also prepared for an exhausting battle. We further had to maintain faith that God would provide the necessary funds for the expedition which cost hundreds of thousands of dollars.

It is easy to receive help from people if you are promoting an evangelistic campaign, but to climb a mountain does not produce the same response. This required great faith. In addition, I suffered from a cardiac disease which the devil had placed on me and with which I had to struggle when I climbed 13 mountains during our training. All kinds of spirits harassed us and tried to make us quit. Within the body of Christ a huge wave of opposition rose up against me. Fortunately God appeased it. The truth is that by the time we reached Nepal and began the war, we were already prepared to believe any kind of miracle. Our faith was unshakeable and that is why we could face all the battles in the war.

The "Chods" which are the worst sorcerers in the world according to the research conducted by George Otis Jr., appeared several times on the glaciers where we camped. They tried to kill us, but could not touch us.

One of our warriors became ill with cerebral edema (water in the brain), when we arrived at the base camp which was 19.000 meters above sea level. All night we fought to save his life as he remained within a high altitude hyperbaric chamber. God's power manifested and he was victoriously healed although he had to immediately descend to the intercession camp, directed by Doris Wagner, which was located at 13.000 feet.

Before we reached our objective, where the site of the throne of darkness was located, the devil launched a horrible lethal attack against us in the form of an avalanche. It came directly towards us and brought down half of the mountain with it. But God's hand manifested in an awesome manner. A crevice opened in the ice right before us and swallowed the avalanche. Not a hair on our heads was touched. Praise the Lord! To tell about all the attacks of the evil one and how the power of Jesus neutralized them one by one, would occupy an entire book. What I want to say about warfare is that it takes faith, resistance, understanding, sanctity, much courage and a readiness to give your life. When we look at the results, which are not always immediate, we see that entire cities receive the gospel, and that the glory of God becomes manifest in the darkest places of the world. There is nothing more gratifying than that!

4. We have fought in the heavenly realms and have overcome.

Definitely God is calling His faithful and chosen ones to fight the great battles of the end times with Him in order to deliver the nations. We have fought and we have overcome. The war is real. It is dangerous, but it is worth fighting for the freedom of the captives.

To be a part of the army, it is not necessary to be perfect or extremely mature in the knowledge of spiritual warfare. In order to participate in a battle at this level, it is necessary to fight in accordance with the order and requirements that I have discussed in this book. With the correct covering and correct strategy, the grace of God will supply your needs and He will continue to perfect you until you have become a great warrior.

The truly courageous ones of Jehovah, who are consecrated to His glory, as He says in Isaiah 13, are very special to the heart of God. Fighting for the Supreme Majesty of the universe is one of the greatest privileges which we can aspire for.

The soldiers of God, those from whom He can ask anything at any price, are the true bride of the Lamb and there are magnificent rewards set aside for them. Our intimate communion with Him in worship is relevant for our formation and development as the army of God.

I want to encourage all the courageous people of God, those whose priorities are no longer the comforts and possessions of this world, but only God. Let us lift together the banner of His army and let us train thousands of soldiers who are waiting for us.

All over the world there are true warriors who may go unnoticed in their churches, but whose hearts beat for the liberation of their cities. They are waiting to hear and see people who are full of courage and truth and who can serve as role models for them so they can rise up as well. Let us stop the waves of fear that intimidate the children of God and show the church the real power of our infallible God.

> *"For God hath not given us the spirit of fear; but of power, and of love, and of a sound mind."*
> *- 2 Timothy 1:7*

Training

For your training I recommend you study the books from authors who have a great understanding about this subject matter. I myself have a book which is used in many Bible institutes to teach spiritual warfare called: "Shaking the Heavens", I also recommend my books: "Regions of Captivity", "Iniquity" and the "Dark Secret of G.A.O.T.U".

We have also produced spiritual and territorial warfare documentaries that will help you enormously on how to implement in practice a spiritual war. Additionally, we have produced a series of video and audio teachings to the ends of providing training in these areas.

Voice of The Light Ministries

Visit our website

www.voiceofthelight.com

Write to:
Voice of The Light Ministries
P. O. Box 3418
Ponte Vedra, FL 32004
United States of America

Contact us online:
www.voiceofthelight.com/contact-us/

Follow us on **FACEBOOK** & **TWITTER**
Watch us on **Frequencies of Glory TV** & **YOUTUBE**

www.frequenciesofglorytv.com

www.youtube.com/user/VoiceoftheLight

www.facebook.com/AnaMendezFerrellFanPage

www.twitter.com/AnaMendezF

Made in the USA
Monee, IL
24 October 2021